ROXANE
GAY
BO☐KS

THE ANSWER IS IN THE WOUND

Also by Kelly Sundberg

Goodbye, Sweet Girl

THE ANSWER IS IN THE WOUND

TRAUMA, RAGE, AND ALCHEMY

KELLY SUNDBERG

New York

Copyright © 2025 by Kelly Sundberg

All rights reserved. No part of this book may be reproduced in any form or by any electronic or mechanical means, including information storage and retrieval systems, without permission in writing from the publisher, except by a reviewer, who may quote brief passages in a review. Scanning, uploading, and electronic distribution of this book or the facilitation of such without the permission of the publisher is prohibited. Please purchase only authorized electronic editions, and do not participate in or encourage electronic piracy of copyrighted materials. Your support of the author's rights is appreciated. Any member of educational institutions wishing to photocopy part or all of the work for classroom use, or anthology, should send inquiries to Grove Atlantic, 154 West 14th Street, New York, NY 10011 or permissions@groveatlantic.com.

Sara Ahmed, "Hearing Complaint," in *Complaint!*, pp. 1–26. Copyright 2021, Duke University Press. All rights reserved. Republished by permission of the copyright holder, and the Publisher. www.dukeupress.edu.

From *Waking the Tiger: Healing Trauma* by Peter A. Levine, published by North Atlantic Books, copyright © 1997 by Peter A. Levine. Reprinted by permission of North Atlantic Books.

By Stevie Smith, from *All the Poems*, copyright © 1937, 1938, 1942, 1950, 1957, 1962, 1966, 1971, 1972 by Stevie Smith. Copyright © 2016 by the Estate of James MacGibbon. Copyright © 2015 by Will May. Reprinted by permission of New Directions Publishing Corp.

The Collected Poems and Drawings of Stevie Smith by Stevie Smith, copyright © 2018. Reprinted by permission of publisher Faber and Faber Ltd.

Any use of this publication to train generative artificial intelligence ("AI") technologies is expressly prohibited. The author and publisher reserve all rights to license uses of this work for generative AI training and development of machine learning language models.

The events and experiences that I write about are all true and have been faithfully rendered as I remember them. In some places, I've changed the names, identities, and other specifics of individuals who have played a role in my life in order to protect their privacy. The conversations I re-create come from my clear recollections of them, through they are not written to represent word-for-word transcripts. In all instances, I've retold them in a way that evokes the feeling and meaning of what was said, always keeping with the true essence of the exchanges.

FIRST EDITION

Printed in the United States of America

This book was set in 13-pt. Centaur MT by Alpha Design & Composition of Pittsfield, NH.

First Grove Atlantic hardcover edition: August 2025

Library of Congress Cataloging-in-Publication data is available for this title.

ISBN 978-0-8021-6425-4
eISBN 978-0-8021-6426-1

Roxane Gay Books
an imprint of Grove Atlantic
154 West 14th Street
New York, NY 10011

Distributed by Publishers Group West

groveatlantic.com

25 26 27 28   10 9 8 7 6 5 4 3 2 1

This book is dedicated to Teddy and Bob.
Pets mean so much to single moms, and mine got me through many lonely days and nights. I am grateful to have found two of the loves of my life when I needed them most.

"Pain that gets performed is still pain."
—Leslie Jamison

"*Disavowal*, says the silence."
—Maggie Nelson

May this book be an exorcism.

Contents

Introduction	1
His Apologies in Erasure	11

Part 1: Captivity

It Was Once like This Before	17
Mornings, on the Ranch	20
Mates	23
The Sharp Point in the Middle	41
You Are the Star	54
The Sun Is at the Beginning of the House	59

Part 2: Rupture

Whirling Disease	71
Poppies	80
No, You	93
Spoons	101
Everything That Brings Me Joy Also Brings Me Sorrow Now	107

Part 3: The Problem

Silences	113
Still Screaming	119

Winter's Burden	125
The Problem	130
When You Blame Amber Heard, You Blame Me Too	136
Where Were the Mothers like Me?	141
Everything That Brings Me Joy Also Brings Me Sorrow Now	151

Part 4: Love & Rage

The Witching Hour	157
Every Line Is a Scream	168
Ritchie County Mall	178
Couplet	190
My Mother, My Self, and I	198
Everything That Brings Me Joy Also Brings Me Sorrow Now	206

Part 5: After

Gifts	213
The Answer Is in the Wound	222
Victim Impact Statement	233
The Blue of Melancholy	240
You Are the Star	247
How to Not Be Heartbroken	250
Acknowledgments	261
Bibliography	265

THE ANSWER IS IN THE WOUND

Introduction

When I was twenty-four, I went into the wilderness seeking transcendence. I had been raised by a gentle forester father in an outdoors community in the rural American West, where transcendental narratives of wilderness as salvation were normal. John Muir spoke of two pines as a doorway to a new world, and like so many others before me, I sought access to that new world through my retreat from civilization.

What was I retreating from? I didn't really know. It's nearly impossible to articulate a sense of persistent dissatisfaction and malaise, but that was where I was at. In rural Idaho, I felt like an outsider. Even in the early twenty-first century, Idaho wasn't a friendly place for women, and I had spent my lifetime watching men *do things* while women stayed home.

My hometown was predominantly Mormon, and most of the women I knew were homemakers. They stayed at home, took care of the children, and worked to maintain the appearances of their families, their reputations, and their bodies. It's a stereotype, but sometimes, stereotypes exist for a reason, and the Mormon women *looked* a certain way. Thin, with clear skin, white teeth, and straight hair. Maybe this was because they avoided substances, even the benign ones like caffeine. Maybe it was because, by and large, they had money. Maybe it was because the expectations were so strong that they would do whatever they had to in order to look good.

I remember my friend's mother taking drugs to lose weight that were later outlawed. She would get a perm, then straighten her hair every day. The perm was purportedly "for body," but all I knew was that, after all of that work, her hair looked like the hair on a LEGO person. She baked her own bread and made all of her food from scratch, but she also spent long afternoons in her darkened bedroom with migraines. As my friend and I grew older, and I leaned more into becoming who I really wanted to be, my friend's mother told her that she was no longer allowed to be friends with me because I wasn't Mormon, and that hurt me deeply.

The mythology of the hero's quest was alive and well in Idaho, but as a woman, there were few models for me to follow, so I followed the models of men. I wanted to wear my Vans with dresses. I wanted to cut my hair into a pixie cut. I wanted tattoos and a nose ring. More than that, I wanted to have adventures. I wanted to do work that felt meaningful and important. I wanted to be independent. I wanted to be *free*.

It was the desire for freedom that compelled me to accept a job working for the US Forest Service as a wilderness ranger. A backcountry plane flew me into a remote airstrip and dropped me off at Indian Creek Guard Station in the Frank Church Wilderness. As I sat on the porch of my Forest Service cabin, I heard the words in my head: "This is a story of a woman who went into the wilderness and came out unchanged." I was lonely in the wilderness, and it turned out that the silence didn't make my thoughts more wise or prophetic. The solitude didn't bring me closer to God; it only made me miserable.

Growing up in a rural, patriarchal community led to that dissatisfaction and malaise that led me to that job. Even as a child, I was outspoken, fiery, and smart. "She's got that redheaded temper," they said (because everyone knows who *they* are in a small community). "She's too smart for her own good," *they* also said. In high school, *they* made assumptions about my sexuality, did things like scrawl the words "Fucking Dyke" over a picture of me that was tacked to a bulletin board. I didn't retreat; I bit back. *They* were unfazed, and I was miserable.

For a girl who grew up poor in the rural American West, there weren't a lot of opportunities to leave. I dreamed of traveling the world, of working in New York City, but those were just dreams. My reality was that I would have to stay. Migration, in the traditional sense of the word, wasn't an option for those of us who grew up with a lack of resources and education—even for the smartest of us. Our migrations often happened in the spiritual realm. We accessed our "spirit guides" as a way of finding tolerance for our lives. Our reality was that, though progressive politics wasn't yet a thing in the rural American West, white New Age mysticism was alive and well.

In high school, I worked at a local bookstore owned by a woman. The store carried books with titles such as *Women Who Run with the Wolves* and *Zen and the Art of Motorcycle Maintenance*. Crystals hung in the windows, a tiny plug-in fountain gurgled next to the cash register, and wooden flute music piped through the speakers. Like every other bookstore at that time, we also carried the book *Men Are from Mars, Women Are from Venus*. My high school English teacher had bought the book, and he would read chapters to us in class. I remember him telling us that it was never too early to learn that men want to be "needed" while women just want to be "cherished." I remember thinking that my English teacher made me uncomfortable. I remember watching him sit on top of a desk in front of the class, then spread his legs wide open as if he sat that way all of the time. I remember thinking that, if I didn't get out of that town, I would never be the person I wanted to be.

When I graduated, the three women I worked with at the bookstore gave me a meditation pillow and my first set of runes. They hugged me and told me to seek guidance from the spirits when I felt lost. They told me that they were so proud of me, that they had so much hope for my future. None of them had been able to finish college, and I knew I was lucky to be going to college at all.

I wanted to go to a progressive liberal arts college in the Midwest, but my family couldn't afford it, so I landed at the University of Montana in Missoula, which was the closest "city" (population: 58,000) in miles to my hometown, but it was geographically difficult to access. First, we had to drive up, then down a winding mountain pass that crossed the Continental Divide and two mountain ranges—the Beaverheads and the Bitterroots. In many ways, Missoula felt like home, but in other ways, it felt foreign. There were students like me—students who had grown up in the impoverished local communities of Montana and Idaho—and there were students the locals referred to as "Granuppies" (granola + yuppie). The Granuppies had come from the East Coast to have the exotic experience of studying in the Rocky Mountains. When I told the Granuppies I had grown up in Idaho, they peppered me with questions, always curious what it was like to actually live in that region. They commented on how beautiful the nature was, and I found myself building up that aspect of my upbringing; I was too proud to admit I had been miserable in such a pristine place.

Here is the thing about towns with economies that rely on the land: The land isn't as beautiful as it is utilitarian. My county had an economy that was dependent on mining, cattle ranching, and logging. By the time I was in high school, federal lawsuits from environmental groups had shut down most of the logging, and my family bore the weight of the community's anger. My father was the representative from the US Forest Service who had to tell the logging companies there would be no more clear-cutting, and when I was in high school, he received death threats on our family's answering machine. The neighbors had signs in their windows that read, THIS HOUSE SUPPORTED BY TIMBER DOLLARS. Those signs felt directed at us, and the realities of their homes were such that it was obvious that support wasn't paying their bills.

Those neighbors were poor. Poorer than us, at least, and in a community that was so small, so angry, and so desperate, the folks who weren't hungry were "rich." To be rich was to be contemptible, and it would be dishonest of me if I didn't admit I had internalized that mindset. In Missoula, I envied the ease of the Granuppies' lives, but I didn't respect them, and no matter how much I meditated or consulted my runes, the spirits didn't give me guidance on how to reconcile such extreme class disparities. I dropped out of the University of Montana after one semester and returned to my hometown. Between three jobs, I worked seventy-hour weeks in the service industry while living in my parents' basement. This was not the life I had envisioned for myself, so when I had the opportunity to work for the Forest Service, I took it. It was an easy decision. In rural Idaho, working for the Forest Service was one of the few ways to make a living wage, and beyond that, I would experience the wilderness as it was meant to be experienced.

During my one semester at the University of Montana, my freshman composition instructor had themed her class around wilderness. We'd read Edward Abbey and Henry David Thoreau, and I'd learned that wilderness could both heal and restore the spirit. No one was freer than Abbey and Thoreau had been, and I believed that, if I followed their paths, I, too, would be independent and wise. The wisdom would show me that I needed no one, and if I didn't need anyone, then it didn't matter that I didn't fit in.

I'd grown up in a strict Christian family but had stopped being a believer in my early teen years. Still, the spiritualist in me craved nature's transcendence. I often thought of a print on my neighbor's wall. It was called *Footsteps*, and had a painting of footsteps in the sand, along with a dialogue between Jesus and an unnamed person. Jesus told the person he would always walk beside them, but the person asked why there was only one pair of footsteps in the sand during the toughest times?

Jesus answered, "Because those were the times when I carried you." The picture was cheap, and the sentiment trite, but, still, I looked at those footprints in the sand and yearned to be carried.

At Indian Creek, I spent a lot of time alone, but I also spent more time with men than ever before. There was the trail crew that came in after weeklong hitches in the woods, the backcountry pilots who popped into my office to chat with me, and the river guides who led guided trips down the Salmon River. Those trips billed themselves as offering the "full wilderness experience." For a mere $2,000, tourists could float through sixty miles of wilderness while dining on fresh seafood in the evenings and participating in group-led beach yoga in the mornings. The river guides were good-looking, tanned, and charming. The trail crew, rugged and rough. The pilots, surprisingly intellectual. Being the only woman in a forest full of men meant that I got a lot of attention—mostly unwanted. After killing a nest of baby mice for me, one of the trail crew guys asked if he could sleep in my cabin that night. I said no and locked my door. One river guide told me that, as a "woman in a certain industry," my role in the wilderness was to let men into my bed. Another river guide said I could be "pretty if I tried." I was so tired, by then, and started crying. He got flustered. "I know it must be hard," he said, not unkindly. I'm not sure what he thought was hard. I didn't know how to tell him that I wasn't crying out of sadness; I was crying out of anger.

And then, finally, there was the co-worker who talked constantly about his ex-wife. He called her a bitch and told me that he'd been arrested for pulling a gun on her. Still, he complimented me, said that I was nothing like her, that I was "soft" and "sweet." I enjoyed his praise: I didn't take the time to think about what it meant that he abused his wife. At one point, I complained about the other men, and he said, "Don't listen to those men. They don't deserve a second of your time."

"Thank you for being nice to me," I said.

He looked down, embarrassed, then back up. "Girl, you're easy to be nice to," he replied.

And I was. Somewhere between the first river guide, and the trail crew member, and the next river guide, I had learned how to be a woman that *was easy to be nice to.*

My boss was a woman, an Amazonian, psychic redhead named Sheri. She flew in occasionally to check on me, and perhaps it was her stature—she towered over most of the men—but they cowered beneath her. They hated her, but also respected her. Sheri was gruff—known for being difficult and opinionated—but she was also kind. One night, we sat on the porch of my cabin, and she laid out a spread of tarot cards. "You're smart," she said, "but you're going to have to get tougher."

I understood what she meant. I had gone into the wilderness seeking the experience of a Granuppie or one of those tourists who paid to float the river in comfort, but instead, I was having the experience of a working-class woman on the job.

Transcendence would have been easy to find if I was rich, I thought.

But I wasn't rich. I was a woman trying to exist in a man's world and no amount of meditation or divination was going to change that. Only I could change that, so I did. It took me a long time. I went back to college. I moved out of Idaho. I graduated from three state schools with an MFA, a PhD, and a mortgage-sized amount of student loans. I got married, had a child, lived through an abusive marriage and painful divorce, then became a single parent. I became tougher, harder. No longer soft or sweet, I was kind, but not nice, and I chose not to care if I was *easy to be nice to*.

On the night of the 2016 election, when America elected a man like my former co-workers, like my ex-husband, and like so many other men I had known in my lifetime—and when my hometown in Idaho went overwhelmingly red while I lived across the country in Ohio—I curled up with my feelings of betrayal on my bathroom floor and sobbed as quietly as possible. I didn't want my son to hear me, so like all of the other women I knew, I picked myself up off the floor.

I went to bed and held the rose quartz I keep on my bedside table. Rose quartz is purported to help with love, particularly feelings of self-love. In the same way that I no longer believed that wilderness could save me, I didn't really believe in the power of the crystal, but I believed in the power of beauty. By then, my father and I had hiked into the Bob Marshall Wilderness in Montana, the most inaccessible wilderness in the lower 48. We climbed seven thousand feet in our first day of hiking. At the summit, my father took a picture of me standing in front of a field of bear grass. In it, I am smiling. When I look at that picture, I hear my father's words when we reached the top. He said, "I had no idea that you were so strong."

I had no choice. This world dictated that I had to be strong. There was no spirit who was going to carry me through difficult times. Those footsteps in the sand had to be my own, and that was as close to transcendence as I would ever get.

I'm telling you all of this because this essay collection isn't about where I grew up (though there are aspects of that here) or about how I learned to be strong within that context (my memoir covers those aspects of my life). This essay collection is about a different kind of journey—a journey of recovery from abuse. The context of my life matters because the girl I was then became the woman I am now.

I have been shaped by trauma. At times, it has felt like I have disappeared inside of it, but that girl, the one who knew how to be strong, was always inside of me. She told me to lean back into the spirituality, even if it was a little woo-woo, that I had learned from strong women when I was a teenager. She told me not to be too "nice." She told me to fight for my autonomy. She told me that I had survived hard things, and I could survive them again. She told me that I could be free.

These essays are written to be stand-alone pieces, but they are also arranged to be read in order. The arrangement is a map. The destination is hope.

His Apologies in Erasure

Original Source: My ex-husband's apology emails from when we were still married.

I ▮ know ▮▮▮
▮▮ I get mad. ▮▮ I'm mad ▮▮
I'm hurt ▮▮ I have ▮▮▮ rage.
▮ everything feeds into me ▮▮

I'm scared ▮▮ of losing you. I love my life ▮▮ and
▮▮▮ I tell you how
awful you are. ▮▮ That is abusive of me ▮
▮▮▮ I've been too hard
on you ▮▮
▮▮▮

▮ I love my life ▮▮ ▮ I ▮ dreamed it
could be. ▮▮ possible. ▮
▮ because of the joy ▮▮ I don't tell
you ▮

▮▮ I'm sorry. ▮
▮▮
▮▮

I'm sorry I didn't trust you
I'm very scared I'm
afraid of others' reactions I blame you

I just can't handle any sort of criticism.

I'm sorry

I'm sorry
I make you feel worthless and alone

I know

it broke

you

I'm going to devote part of my time

with my rage.

You're right to think about leaving.

Sometimes I'm incredibly filled with pride and vanity

I love it that you're such a devoted wife to me. I love that you have always seen the best in me

I also love you because you've always forgiven me

I tell you

these are my real feelings for you.

I haven't been appreciating you I'm sorry

███████████████ it was all my fault. I'm sorry. ████
███████████████ I'm sorry ████████████████████
██████ all the hurt ██████████████████████
█████████████████████ I want ████ I want ████
██
███████████████████████ you, and how much you support me. Thank you for ███ giving █████ me █████ you.

PART 1

CAPTIVITY

It Was Once like This Before

It was once like this before. Not enough to mention. Not enough to disregard.

I thought—*We are not of the same class; we could never marry*—but I am already married to a man who writes of killing puppies with a stone. It is a mercy I do not understand because I have never personally seen him kill a puppy.

Now I am going to tell you a story of a girl who drank wine from a trash can in a plastic house (it was me). This story is true or maybe not—I appropriate often. The wine was homemade apple; the glass was a measuring cup. One cup was generous. One half cup was lonely.

This house: It was made to look like wood. Lovely home, I said (but I didn't mean it).

Now I am going to tell you a story of a man named Lyle. He was kicked in the head by a horse. This story is true. He shook when he spoke, or spooked, or stuttered. He told me about Jesus (or Judas), who was only fulfilling his destiny. God betrayed him. It was not the other way around.

He also told me I had lovely teeth. Like snow. Or frost. People are so predictable, I said.

Now I am going to tell you a story of a pregnant stripper in a boat. This story is true. No appropriations. She told me about a woman who held an apple in her mouth while her lover kissed the backs of her thighs. It made her so sick.

I stared at the pregnant stripper. That is not my child, I said. Of course not (she told me), you already have a child. You tell him how special he is, too often. He will grow up with narcissistic tendencies. You will love him, worship him, but he will have little regard for you.

Still, that is not what we are talking about now.

We are talking about a little girl who stepped onto a dark balcony (it was me). Foot landed on softness. Squishy. Such a childish word for dying—for a kitten.

She asked me (that pregnant stripper), what is it you want to write about? I told her I want to write about sadness or poverty.

But you can't (she told me); because the absolute value of sadness is sadness, and the absolute value of poverty is sadness. They are the same distance from zero on the number line.

I held that tiny kitten in my hand—its heart exposed—beating rapidly—and I cried and cried and cried. No. I won't, I said. I won't hold this heart in my hand.

The Answer Is in the Wound

I know
it broke

you

Mornings, on the Ranch

Frost splinters across trampled earth, and an irrigation ditch carves a pathway through the dark, frozen mud saturated with urine and manure: heaping, wet piles of manure that fall—*plop, plop, plop!*—leaving steam that floats into the cold air where it dissipates before it ever meets the sky. The steam hovers in a gauzy haze just above waist level while my gloved hands tuck into the curves of my elbows, seeking warmth in the down-enclosed folds.

Mornings, on Celinne's ranch, begin at 5 a.m. At my house, I sleep until 8 a.m., then rush to catch my bus to middle school at 8:30, but here, Celinne's mom flicks on the light at 4:45 a.m., and soon, Celinne nudges me out of bed, telling me I have to help milk the cows. The house is warm, too warm, and we each select a pair of crusty, oversized boots—shitkickers, they are—and tromp out to the dairy barn. *Tromp, tromp, tromp!* Our shitkickers break the eerie winter silence. It is a winter for praying, for giving thanks, for bread, and for milk—hot, steamy milk that pours forth—that tastes so much sweeter than the white, homogenized water Mom buys in a big plastic jug with a blue lid.

I don't like milk. Never have. Years later, I will learn why. *Lactose intolerance.* Such a shameful term on the ranch. There is a lot of shame on the ranch. Celinne's mom prods me to drink my milk with a smile that doesn't quite meet her eyes. I sip the white, viscous liquid, still warm, sugary sweet. Fresh milk is the best milk, she says, but I hide my gag reflex behind my hand, forcing the creamy mixture down my throat.

Then we pray, our hands linked across the table, heads bowed, while the sun rises behind the mountains. We pray for a good winter, for good milk, for prosperity. Ranching is hard work. Except on Sunday. Sunday is the day of rest, when ranchers go to church, and people weep and hold up their hands yelling "Praise God!" while their bodies sway in reptilian motions. I ask my mom why we don't do that at *our* church, but Mom just says Lutherans worship differently. *Quietly*. And Lutherans don't think it's a sin to ride in cars with boys.

Celinne's not allowed to ride in cars with boys, not even my brother, who's eighteen and suffers through picking me up at school and volleyball practice after he finishes work bagging groceries at the IGA. He just bought his first car—a lumbering, decade-old Chevrolet—a "grandpa" car, I say. If I knew better, I would call it a "pimp" car, but I don't know that term yet. The seats are plush, brown velvet, the color of chocolate. Or manure.

Liquid manure that slides down the concrete floor while Celinne fastens the shining stainless steel suction cups to the swollen udders of calm cows lined up in a row, tails swinging. She flicks a switch, *flick!*, then the pulsing starts and frothy whiteness slides through tubes, landing silently in an innocuous stainless steel canister in the corner.

Celinne's a good girl. She never complains about the early mornings or hard work. She prays every night, and when I stay over, we kneel next to each other, our hands pointing heavenward, *this is the church. this is the steeple!* She never complains about her parents, who are older than my parents, who don't let her watch PG movies or talk to boys.

I don't complain when she stays at my house in town. Morning has long passed, the day stretching into dusk. My brother and his friends play basketball, and Celinne chases them, jumping on their backs, pressing her budding breasts into their muscles. I don't complain when the sky turns black, and Celinne is in the backseat of my brother's car, sinking into those brown depths with my brother's best friend while the car is parked in the driveway. Is it riding with a boy if the car isn't moving? My brother and I stand next to each other, both slightly sickened, the age difference between us growing. First, it's five years, now it's ten, now it's twenty, and still, I'm standing there, watching the car windows steam like the hot manure on icy ground. *I'm just a girl*, I think. *I'm not ready for night to arrive.*

Mates

Sun Valley, Idaho, 1998

One of the swans was murdered; he was stabbed in the night. Swans mate for life, so his mate grieved. She lay on the steps of the boardwalk that traced the pond, head bowed into her legs. Tourists approached her tentatively, threw breadcrumbs at her, but she looked up with large, teary eyes, then rested her head back into the billowy down of her feathers. One afternoon, I sat on a step beside her and watched the pond. She lifted her head toward me when I sat down. Her eyes, large and damp, sparkled. Painful like bright snow. I slid a cracker in front of her, but she pushed it away. She was starving herself to death.

Someone offered a $10,000 reward for the arrest of the person who stabbed her mate.

I thought of the dead swan in the snow, blood spreading through the ice like petals. Death is everywhere during an Idaho winter. I know how blood looks against the glistening whiteness.

Or was it actually two springs before when the swan was stabbed, and I tried to give her a cracker? The spring when my high school classmates and I went to Sun Valley for a school newspaper competition? The spring when I envied all of the pretty girls who had the attention of the boys from the bigger school districts? The spring when I consoled myself that at least I was the smart one? The spring when, even though I was the smart one, I only won an honorable mention in the writing competition I was expected to win? The spring when the announcer gave me my certificate and the word "Superior" had been crossed out?

Instead, someone had scrawled "Honorable Mention" in black marker just below.

How did I end up in Sun Valley nearly two years after graduating from high school? I was the smart one. I was the one who my high school newspaper advisor said would be her Pulitzer Prize winner. I had been in a graduating class of fewer than eighty students, so it wasn't hard to be the smart one, but I left high school flush with expectations.

After graduation, I started college in Montana—the only student from my rural high school to be admitted into an honors college—but I spent the days huddled in my dorm room trying to out-sleep the anxiety, the expectations, the weight of all of the people I knew I was going to disappoint. My grades suffered as a result, and I dropped out two weeks into the second semester when I learned I had been placed on academic probation and could lose my scholarship.

I looked for a cure for my anxiety. I blew my student loans on a trip to Europe. I spent the following summer waitressing in my hometown. I tried living independently in Portland,

Oregon. After all of that, I ended up back on my parents' doorstep.

In Salmon, after moving back from Portland, I ran into Ann, my best friend from childhood. As girls, we spent long days at her house across the street from mine, playing with Barbies, brushing out their hair, coveting their long legs and tan skin.

Her family had a playroom in the basement that was cold and damp. Ann and I huddled underneath hand-knit afghans for warmth; sometimes, we played house—fantasizing of love. Sometimes, Ann pressed me to the wall, pushed her hand over my mouth, and kissed the other side of her hand passionately—with force—the same way we had seen Patrick Swayze kissing Jennifer Grey in *Dirty Dancing*. We played like that until we grew bored of the game, moving on to Hungry Hungry Hippos or Monopoly.

We avoided Dale, her younger brother. He was violent, out of control. He pounded me over the head with a meat tenderizer. He slammed me in the back so hard with a Wiffle bat that the wind formed a bubble in my chest and my face turned red from the pressure. He chased me and pulled my long hair back, so my neck stretched tight.

He hid in the closet and eavesdropped on our private conversations. I got my period when I was only eleven. I sat on Ann's bed and whispered the news to her. She asked what it was like, and I described the humiliation of my mom showing me how to rinse my panties in the bathroom sink—cold water, not hot—and the horror of wearing a pad in public, convinced that someone could see it. Dale burst out of the closet laughing and pointing. He ran out of the room shouting, "Kelly's got her period! Kelly's got her period!" My cheeks flushed red, and I ran across the street, threw myself on my bed, and cried while my mom watched.

Dale skulked, lurking around corners, hiding behind shadows. Even the bathroom wasn't free from his gaze. Their bathroom in the basement had a hole in the door where a doorknob should have been. Sometimes, when I was peeing, I would look over and see Dale's eye pressed to the hole, his fleshy cheeks protruding through the gap, eye bulging, and I'd scream, "Dale, stop being gross!"

Ann told me about a job in Sun Valley as a lift operator at the ski hill. It only paid minimum wage, but housing and meals were provided for a nominal fee. The idea of living in Sun Valley was better than spending the winter trapped in my dead-end hometown, so I packed up and moved three hours over a mountain pass to the neighboring ski town.

The Sun Valley Lodge—a lumbering hulk of a log cabin—sits at the foot of the small resort town, an ice sculpture of a grinning sun sweating in front of the paved turnaround. Across the boardwalk, through the snow-covered lawn, past the man-made pond where the swans—the Sun Valley mascots—glide lazily, is the Sun Valley Inn, a massive stucco hotel built to look like a Swiss chalet. The entire town is enclosed by parking lots, but in the distance, mountains loom over the valley, mansions dotting the winding roads.

Aspens fill hollows in the hills, white wood bends achingly toward the blue sky, and Bald Mountain, an enormous ski hill, dominated by an intricate network of ski lifts, looms over the entire Wood River Valley.

Ernest Hemingway lived and died in Sun Valley. He wrote the majority of *For Whom the Bell Tolls* in room 206 of the Sun Valley Lodge. He later shot himself in a home built in the same style as the lodge. The walls of the lodge are dotted with photos of Hemingway and other celebrities—Marilyn Monroe, Adam West, and local favorite Arnold Schwarzenegger, among others.

Beyond the Sun Valley Lodge and Sun Valley Inn, another town is hidden. The Pit. The Pit also has buildings made to look like Swiss chalets should any unsuspecting tourist stumble upon them, but the insides of those chalets are stuffed with bunk beds and beanbag chairs. The carpet is dirty, and the buildings smell of armpits and bare feet. The Pit is where the employees live. The Pit was where I lived.

Ann and I grew apart in the sixth grade. She had gone on to become a stoner and ended up at the alternative school while I became a bookish nerd, but we reconnected when I left college. Ann's family had imploded by then. Her Mormon mother had an affair with the Baptist preacher. He was excommunicated, and Ann's mom divorced her dad. The preacher broke up with her mom shortly after the divorce, and her mom took to drinking as if she had been doing it her whole life, as if she hadn't been baking cookies and attending day-long church ceremonies for most of my childhood.

Ann, her boyfriend Tim, and I drove to the Oregon coast once. Ann was struggling with depression. She sat in the backseat quietly while Tim sat up front with me. Tim and I chatted about unimportant things as we drove along the winding coastal roads. I tried to pretend as though I wasn't a third wheel, chattering even more than usual. I didn't understand their relationship. They seemed in love, but very sad. I had never dated then, did not yet understand that love could be sad.

We drove all day to find the ocean, then finally decided to take a right in the direction of the ocean and ended up driving on to sand at dusk. Three kids from small-town Idaho, and none of us had ever seen the ocean. We stood and watched the sunset, the light golden on the dark waves that crashed onto the shore. Ann and I rolled up our pants and waded into the water. Tim took our photo. In it, I am leaning forward, laughing, my hair blowing. Ann is upright—an unreadable smile on her face—an irresistible combination of beauty and sadness.

Before we left, I took one last, long look at the sun disappearing behind the waves. I turned back to the car and Tim had scrawled in the wet sand with a stick, "God Was Here."

The following winter, Ann and Tim broke up, and Ann and I started working at the ski hill. There were only a few women working the lifts, and Ann and I were the youngest. The rest of our co-workers were men. The work was tedious, and I stood and watched the ski lifts swing by, floating through blue sky. Occasionally, I stopped the lift to help a child into the seat, but most of the time, I stood and daydreamed.

When the supermodel, Elle Macpherson, wanted to ride the lift while eight months pregnant, I stopped the machine for her while a tanned ski instructor helped her sit down. One of her slender hands rested in his, and the other hand waved at me generously while she smiled through her fur face mask. She was as beautiful in person as she had been on the cover of *Sports Illustrated*. I looked down at myself. I was in an entirely purple uniform that consisted of ski pants, a heavy Bavarian-style sweater, a ski coat, and a matching purple hat with a tassel that swung down into my eyes. I was dumpy.

Another time, I helped load a ski patrol sled. I stood in front of the sled, waiting for the chair to sweep it up, but became distracted when I saw Maria Shriver in line. She was unmistakable in her full-body, Holstein cow–print ski suit. I stared at her, hypnotized by the black splotches on her white suit, while the chair swept both me and the sled away. I clung to the sled, desperately trying not to fall as the chair crawled up the mountain. The ski patrol officer shouted and rushed over to hit the stop button. The chair lurched to a stop, and I fell with a thud into the snow; flakes rose up around me in a poof, landing in my nostrils and eyes. When I stood up and brushed off my face, Maria Shriver leaned over and asked kindly, "Are you okay?" Embarrassed, I nodded yes.

Her husband, Arnold Schwarzenegger, famously had a fondness for redheads. When he came through my lift line, his Viennese ski instructor had me take off my hat. "Ooh," said Schwarzenegger, when he saw my bright red hair. "I like."

I blushed. After that, the other lift operators called me "Schwarzenegger's girl." For the girl who had only ever thought of herself as the "smart one," the attention was secretly heady. No one in Sun Valley cared if I was smart. I could be whoever I wanted to be.

Ann and I befriended a group of international college students, mostly from Australia and New Zealand. They were fun, friendly, and rich. They ate Vegemite and called each other "mates." My windowless dorm room was in a renovated ranch house on the edge of the pit. It had plywood walls and two hard twin beds with a dresser pressed tightly between the bed and the wall by the door. My room was slightly larger than the other rooms, so it was a good room for gatherings. We lined up along the edges of the beds, passing around beer, bowls, tabs, or mushrooms. The walls expanded temporarily—laughter blending into the night air outside—clear, and cold, and hard.

After a while, Ann's brother, Dale, decided to join her in Sun Valley. He, too, got a job as a lift operator. I wasn't happy when he was put into the room next to mine, but he had grown large and awkward, like a child who had outgrown his limbs. Despite all of the years I'd known him, Dale treated me with shyness, shuffling his feet when he spoke to me and lowering his eyes when I met his gaze. Ann, by then, had thrown herself into a relationship with a young Australian and showed no interest in hanging out with Dale, and Dale no longer resembled the malicious boy of my childhood, so I couldn't help but feel sorry for him.

One night, when I was lying down for bed, I heard Dale leave his room. The plywood separating our living spaces was the cheapest variety available, and I could hear most of what happened on the other side. I was still awake when Dale came back, the door slamming behind him. I pulled a pillow over my ears to block out the sound, but after a few minutes, claustrophobia set in, and I let the pillow slip to the side. His light switch came on, and a faint glow peeped through a knotty hole in the plywood located above eye level. I heard the sound of bottles opening.

The next morning I saw empty malt liquor bottles in the trash. It was an intimacy I didn't want to share with him.

In the confines of the Sun Valley village, a regular rotation of tanned millionaires in fur coats glide along the boardwalk, stopping to watch bonbons being hand-dipped into chocolate or to toss a few crumbs to the swans. In the Pit, we ate their leftovers, but for us too, every night was a party.

After we finished eating, we got high, then went for a swim in the heated outdoor pool. The steam from the pool merged into the cold winter air while we hung from the sides, our heads light from the heat, the flirting, and the marijuana.

Sun Valley was different from Salmon. In high school, my cross-country team traveled to the public school in Sun Valley for a meet. It was the first time most of us had seen this neighboring town. We drooled at the mansions as our thirty-year-old bus farted and burped up the highway. When we reached their school, the building wasn't sinking into a swamp like ours. They didn't have to tow cars out of the mud in the spring because they had sunk up to their bumpers. The track was paved and lacked puddles. The bleachers weren't caving in. But the biggest difference was how the runners looked in their shiny uniforms and new shoes. Standing at the starting line, I looked down at my uniform in embarrassment. My jersey number was made out of electrical tape. The original number had washed off long ago.

This was before I learned I was only an honorable mention when I thought I had been a winner.

Ann and I danced late into the snowy, starry nights. The Kiwis and Australians went to clubs at night, and we went with them. We danced at Bruce Willis's club, the Mint, bought expensive cocktails, and watched for glimpses of ourselves on the big-screen television above the stage. A night at the Mint meant I needed to live off a box of Grape Nuts for the rest of the week, but it was worth it.

A guy named Smitty with a long, stringy ponytail who proudly boasted that he had lived and worked in the Pit for twenty years had a side business giving loans to young girls like me who partied their paychecks away, so whenever I ran out of money, I knocked on his door. He didn't even charge interest. I only had to give him some extra attention in line at the cafeteria, which meant a long, full-body hug after I paid the two dollars for my employee meal. I was discovering the power that came from being young and pretty enough. Not pretty enough to turn heads, but pretty enough.

One night, as I stripped down the layers of my work clothes—boots, wool socks, ski pants, ski sweater, and long underwear—I pulled my tight duo fold top over my head. It hooked on my head, so I yanked, the fabric stretching my eyes tightly upward in the process. As I looked up, I saw an eye pressed to the hole in the wall, fleshy cheek bulging. The eye looked down upon me, scanning the room back and forth nervously.

I screamed and threw my arms across my chest. The eye quickly disappeared. My roommate told my supervisor, and Dale was quietly dismissed. Someone came in and nailed a board over the hole, but I shivered every time I saw it, every time I remembered his nighttime ritual, every time I realized how thin the wall that divided us was.

At the bar one night, I drank too much beer to drive home. The ski patrol bought a keg, and although I was not twenty-one, the bartender didn't check my ID. Another lift operator, a man who wore turtlenecks, had been flirting with me. I was not attracted to him, but I enjoyed the attention. No one had ever paid attention to me like that before.

I couldn't drive home, and he offered to share a cab. We stopped at my building first, and he wanted to walk me in—just to make sure I got in okay, he said, but when he got out of the car, he paid the cab driver. I was confused, but too tipsy to ask questions. He walked me to my door, and I let myself in. He followed.

Then, he was on top of me. The smell of beer and dryer sheets. I wasn't a virgin, but I had only had sex once.

The thin plywood walls rescued me this time. Another man heard and banged on the door. "Time to go, buddy," he yelled.

The man in the turtleneck left.

In the morning, I found my tampon in the sheets next to me—a blossom-like stain around it, like red in the snow.

For the first time, I knew how it felt to be held down.

Soon, Ann's ex-boyfriend Tim moved into Dale's old room. Ann seemed okay with it. She was in love with her handsome Australian. We were convinced Tim had followed her to Sun Valley, but he left her alone, so it didn't bother her.

I had never told Tim, but I had a crush on him when he first moved to Idaho from California in the eighth grade. He had a floppy bowl cut and skateboard. At the eighth grade prom, no one asked me to dance, so I sat in a chair next to Tim, my legs stretched out onto the chair in front of me. I wore a pleated miniskirt and bare legs. I twirled my feet in front of me out of boredom. When I looked up, I caught Tim staring at my thigh. For a moment, I didn't move it. Instead, I looked at him, boldly. He looked back. He wasn't scared, but I was. I quickly pulled my legs down and tucked my shins under my chair.

Later, he took my best friend in high school on a date to a movie at the Roxy, the only movie theater in our one-stoplight town. She was Mormon, so her mom would only allow her to go if I accompanied her. I wished that Tim had asked me to the movie instead of my friend, but they never went out again, and, in time, I forgot about my crush on him.

I was relieved when he moved into Dale's room. I could trust Tim. In the mornings, I knocked on his door to wake him up, and gave him time to dress while I made coffee. I filled a cup for him too, and we drove together to the ski hill.

On Valentine's Day, I opened my door and found a rose on the floor. My heart sank. I picked it up and knocked on Tim's door. "Did you leave this?" I asked.

He shrugged and smiled. "Nope, it wasn't me," he said.

I handed him his coffee and tried not to think about where the rose had come from. The man who wore turtlenecks hadn't forgotten me. He skied by my lift, but I hid in the shack. I could see him peering in, but it was one-way glass. My lift partner asked, "Why don't you like that guy? He's interested in you."

I stared at the coffee mug in my hands and shrugged. "I don't know; I just don't."

I'd never known shame like that before. It was a kind of shame I couldn't articulate. I knew rationally that I hadn't done anything wrong, but in my chest, my heart, I felt as though I had been dirtied somehow. No, I felt as though I had dirtied myself somehow.

I slipped the rose into my bag and put it out of my mind. That night, I returned to my room and changed into my pajamas. I was just readying to turn off the light when I heard a scratching outside the door. My hand froze above the light switch, my heart beating. I stood very still.

There was a knock at the door. I didn't answer. Another knock, then Tim's voice. "Kelly, it's Tim."

I let my hand slip down in relief and opened the door. I was surprised to see him standing in front of me, drunk. He leaned forward, glassy-eyed. "Can I come in?" he asked.

I stood aside, and he came in and sat down on the narrow bed.

"I have something to tell you," he said.

I sat down next to him. "Okay."

He looked at me, then looked down at his hands. He told me about how he had been working on a fishing boat in Alaska before moving to Sun Valley, how he had befriended an alcoholic with liver disease, how they had to work so hard that they would do lines of cocaine to get through the long shifts on the trawler, how they would drink themselves to sleep on their days off. He told me how his father had been an alcoholic, how he had left his friend in Alaska knowing he was going to die.

He started to sob, so I hugged him, and he soaked my shoulder with tears, his back shaking.

He pulled back and looked at me. His eyes scared me.

I grabbed a pillow and scooped it into my lap, hugging it to my chest. I wanted protection from his pain. "That sounds awful," I said.

He nodded. "There was so much anger and hate on the boat. Everyone wanted to kick everyone else's ass. I just wanted to stay out of it. I just wanted to have a good time."

I looked at my hands clutching the pillow. "I know that feeling," I said.

He reached over and took my hand. "When I got home, all I could think of every day was how I wanted to die. Life seemed so hopeless. I had a gun.

"But then I got here, and I saw your smiling face." He smiled at me then, his face still teary.

I nodded my head—shoulders tense—finally understanding. "Did you give me the flower?"

He smiled again. "Of course it was me."

His shoulders straightened. "Now, every morning, I want to wake up, because I know I'll see your face. At least I have that. You give me a reason to wake up."

I was sick. I had so much of my own darkness right then.

"Tim," I said. "I don't know what to say to that."

He looked disappointed. "It's okay," he said. "Really."

I stood up. I just wanted him to leave.

"Okay then, well I need to get up in the morning—" I said. "So I should probably go to bed."

Tim went to the door. He stopped at the door, and turned back to me. "Can I just spend the night here?" he asked.

I thought of the turtleneck man, but I didn't know how to say no. "I don't know," I hedged.

"Can I sleep on your floor?" he asked. "I just want to be close to you."

"Okay," I said, relenting.

I turned off the light and climbed into bed. Tim curled up on the floor next to me, and I lay in the dark, listening to him breathe. He wasn't sleeping either.

The room was pitch-black. I knew he would never hurt me, but still, I was afraid. And ashamed. I don't know what I was ashamed of. I hadn't done anything wrong, but it felt like I had, and I couldn't be his reason to live.

I had to leave.

I was a tourist in that life, and that town, too. The party wasn't a party anymore. The next day, I wouldn't be going back to work. I wouldn't be going back to the mountain that loomed over my life, full of money and excess. I wouldn't be going back to my lift shack with a whiteboard in the corner where a ski patroller had scrawled, "Welcome to Spun Valley"—a nod to the cast of *Beverly Hills 90210*, who showed up at a party on New Year's Eve looking for cocaine while I drank champagne, and danced, and laughed. I wouldn't be going back to *that* man—who wore turtlenecks. I'd never be attracted to a man who wears turtlenecks.

I wouldn't be going back to dead swans and plywood walls.

I was going to pack my car up during the day when everyone was working, and I was going to run. I was going to leave it all behind—the holes in the wall, the parties, the wealth. I knew my life needed to move forward.

But it didn't.

Instead, I went home. And a couple of years later, after my heart had been broken by a man who I had thought would love me forever, I let Tim hold me. I let him hold me on the floor of his mother's house, the same way he had wanted to hold me in that dorm room. I let him hold me and hoped that I would grow to want his love, but I didn't. And the next morning, I drove away again.

Shame . . .

Shame is the void left by the stories I still can't tell.

As the Australians would have said, Tim and I had been "mates," but I misled him. I misled him because, in my most vulnerable moments, the version of myself I didn't like continued to return.

* * *

In Sun Valley, on the night when Tim lay on my floor, I wanted the darkness to hold me—to confine me—to wrap around me like a blanket and make me safe. But it didn't.

And the next day, as I drove out of Sun Valley, I left the closeness of the town—the small Wood River winding through aspens, the ordered rows of condos, the grid-like subdivisions, the mansions dotting the hills, and the looming brick of the Sun Valley Lodge—all of them were dots in the distance. My car wound through switchbacks, climbing the steep mountainside of Galena Summit. When I reached the top, I stood at the overlook where I could see the bowls and dips of the valley that stretched for miles, cradled in snow—so clean it seemed limitless. As I looked at the vista before me, I could almost convince myself that Sun Valley wasn't still there—waiting—just beyond that immaculate whiteness.

thank you for ▮ giving ▮ me ▮ you.

The Sharp Point in the Middle

I am familiar with the geography of a bruise. The borders shift. The color stains bright, then fades. Fingerprints like points on a map.

A bruise stretched across the the Corner Store cashier's cheek and jaw. It was nearly black in the middle, blossoming into a velvety purple near the cheekbone and lips. A fairly recent bruise. Any older, and yellow would have circled it like the glow of a solar system. This must have been a two-punch bruise—probably on the bottom of the chin—particularly painful—teeth crashing together, rattling upward. I stood in line at the Corner Store gripping a six-pack of beer, trying not to stare.

Meanwhile, the woman in front of me plopped a can of mandarin oranges on the counter and asked for a pack of Pall Malls. She wore a loose purple tank top, long black cotton skirt, and house slippers. Her greasy black hair was slicked into a ponytail at the nape of her neck, the edges choppy and misshapen. The woman in line stared at the cashier as though it was a challenge. "What happened to your face?" she asked, arms folded. The cashier stared back, jaw clenched. Her hand rose to her face, and she moved her jaw back and forth—click, click. She moved the jaw again. Click. Click. My heart rate accelerated. The mutual stare lingered a little too long. The cashier slowly spit out the words "A horse."

When I was a sweet-toothed eight-year-old, I went to the Corner Store to buy candy. It was the only residential building among rows of ranch houses, located just at the end of my street. My hometown, Salmon—a tourist and agricultural town in the Idaho mountains—was too small and too poor to have "neighborhoods." My family's house, a clean split-level ranch with a tidy yard, was flanked by a faded white house with a falling-down porch and a cage where three snarling dogs lunged at chain-link, and a blue cottage on the other side of a creek that was owned by an outfitter. Tanned river guides set up tents and hammocks in the yard, smoking joints while playing the guitar and laughing long into the starry Idaho nights. With wide, tan forearms and muscular backs, they were all so very handsome.

I headed past them to the Corner Store, a happy girl with braids and a sweaty dime gripped in her palm. I could only buy nine Sour Patch Kids because the tax cost a penny, and the cashier never budged an inch on that extra penny. Her greasy boss watched over her, a rotund, chain-smoking man who wore beach shorts and sandals. He sat to the side of the register smoking and playing cards, a box fan whirring behind him.

That greasy man was in prison for a while. The Feds busted him for operating a counterfeit money ring. This was before

I fell in love with his nephew in the ninth grade. The nephew was a long-haired, pensive-looking boy who never spoke to me, but sometimes gave me rides on his four-wheeler. He drove fast and hit jumps, and I gripped his waist, my entire body pressed along the outline of his back as we hung suspended in air. That boy never knew I was in love with him because I didn't speak to him either. Instead, I lay alone on the floor in front of my stereo listening to "Never Tear Us Apart" by INXS on repeat. With my back pressed to the floor and my knees raised, I traced the outline of his back in the air, making a map of the memory. *Two worlds collided.*

When I turned twelve, I was already pushing a C cup. At my church confirmation and first communion, I wore a beautiful white dress with a deep, scalloped V in the front. My mom pinned the neckline together so I wouldn't have cleavage, but after drinking the bitter wine and eating the dry, tasteless wafer, a fellow churchgoer told me how "beautiful" I looked. A "real woman," he said, his eyes directed at my chest. I knew what he saw. He didn't see the girl already inside of the woman's body, mourning that her body was no longer her own.

By age fourteen, I was a D cup, but I only ever wore giant tee shirts. I didn't want to give the boys any reasons to look down my shirt, and the tees offered ventilation while my friend Pete, a skinny blond with a loud laugh, and I played pool at the sticky Corner Store, trying to escape the summer heat. The pool table stood in the middle of the video section, and we saw what people rented—how some of the men would come in and act like they were going to check out *Young Guns II* before putting the box back on the shelf quickly when they thought no one was looking and asking the cashier for one of the "behind the counter" movies instead while Pete and I snickered.

Pete was already having sex, but I was not, and he liked to remind me of that. Pete had been raised by his divorced mother, and his sex education came from Masters and Johnson. He was the person who instructed me on where the hymen was located. Up to that point, I had been under the impression that it was right at the front of the vagina. I had never personally tried to find it. I didn't believe him until he pulled out his giant book and showed me a map of the female reproductive system. I couldn't argue then with the evidence drawn in a pink diagram before me.

Pete spent the summers living in our town with his dad, an attorney, and he smuggled the book from his mother's house. This was before the convenience of the internet, and we sure as hell weren't going to check out Masters and Johnson from our small-town library. I had already been banned from borrowing "dirty" books. I had recently graduated from Jackie Collins to Bret Easton Ellis, but my mom read the first chapter of *The Rules of Attraction*, then marched down to the library, and forbade them from lending me any more pornographic novels. When I protested, she told me they would give me "unrealistic expectations about love." She was right. They did. I still have an attraction to chaos—to drama—to intense expressions of feeling.

When we weren't playing pool at the Corner Store, we hung out in Pete's dad's basement—a wood-paneled room with a velour sectional couch, a pool table, a fridge, and shelves upon shelves of archived *Playboy* magazines in mint condition that dated back to the fifties. We spent a lot of time flipping through them, but I'm not sure why.

Once, we checked out the movie *Kids* from the Corner Store because it was rated NC-17, and we thought we were being edgy. At the end of the movie, a boy raped a girl who was passed out on a couch. I squirmed, stomach turning, looking down at my lap. I was sitting on the ground, back to the couch, and Pete was sitting above me, legs crossed. We had never been attracted to each other. That was the basis of our friendship. Still, we were pretty normal adolescents. I moved my shoulder from where it had been touching his legs, my skin crawling. Pete spoke up first. "This is making me horny," he said. "How about you?"

"No," I said, looking back at him with disgust. I scooted farther away.

Pete briefly dated my best friend Megan, but she broke up with him before they ever kissed. The night that they were supposed to have their first kiss, he leaned over and asked, "May I kiss you?"

She said no.

She later told me that it was a turn-off that he had asked. We were still very young. We wanted men to be assertive.

I teased Pete about that for years. "Who asks permission for a kiss?" I said.

At school, we were using metal compasses. I loved to press the sharp tip into the white paper, then draw a perfect circle around it in thick gray lead. I drew my own Venn diagrams. This was my life. This was Pete's. This was Megan's. This was yours. This was everything else. I drew my own romance. I saw myself as the sharp point in the middle. The line circled around me, the center of that universe, the beauty of it all contained in the white space.

Around the time that we started high school, a boy named Leif began to silently stalk me. Leif was a pyromaniac, and he was also probably a bit slow, but no one really knew for sure. He built explosives as a hobby. One day, I made the mistake of smiling at him while I was playing pool at the Corner Store. After that, he popped up every time we played. Creeping behind me, he would poke his head over my shoulder. If I jumped, which I always did, he smiled a bit, but he never laughed. He wasn't a laugher.

After scaring me, he went to the arcade portion of the store and played *Duck Hunt*, looking at me intently over the barrel of the plastic gun in between shots.

Target. Sight. Shoot.

Soon, he started talking to me—voice low and urgent. I didn't understand much of what he said. A lot of it had to do with video games, or explosives, but he talked to me as though we were twin souls. I nodded and smiled the way my mother had taught me to. I was a polite girl. I've never been good at saying no, but I've always known how to smile.

Once, while I was playing pool with Megan, Leif burst in, as animated as I had ever seen him. He came to me, hand hidden behind his back, then quickly waved it in my face. I recoiled. His hand, pink and smooth, had fingers that were gray, rotten holes with a circle of skin encasing them. They looked like miniature gravel quarries, getting grayer and deeper with each layer. Leif was proud. He had burned them off with explosives while making fireworks. He smiled as he held the charred fingers out to me. "I won't have fingerprints anymore," he said. "I can do anything I want, and they can't catch me. See? See?"

The minute we finished our game, Megan and I left. We ran the entire way to her house, our laughter so loud we were almost shrieking. When we got to her house, we collapsed into a heap on top of each other in the yard. "What a weirdo," Megan said.

"A total weirdo," I agreed. We laughed again.

"I think I just peed a little," Megan said.

We laughed some more, but then I worried he had heard us. I worried I had hurt his feelings.

Twenty years later, my husband was fingerprinted after his arrest, the ink creating a stained map for future police identification. I loved his fingers—long, slender, gentle fingers that could play the guitar and caress my hair. His fingers also curled into a fist, and maybe I loved that too.

When I tried to fight back, he held me down and spit in my face. Then, he spit in my face again. And then, one more time. It was as though all of those men—that first man who had stared at my body like he owned it, and then the next, and then the next, and finally, the man I married—they were all spitting in my face.

I have this memory. I was standing in the doorway crying. He was lying in the bed. Why was I standing in the doorway? Why was he in the bed? His eyes were like tunnels, and I was running, running, running through them.

He stared at me, then spoke. "Everything bad that you think about yourself. It's all true."

My tears turned into sobs.

"Stop crying," he screamed. "You're acting like a child."

It was a relief when he hit me. When the blows started, the words stopped.

He told me I was ugly. I wanted to be pretty.

Q: How do you love someone who hates you?
A: By hating yourself more.

When we were dating, my husband cheated on me with a friend of his from high school, but I didn't find out until after we married. She was one of many, but she was the one who rattled me. "Why," I asked him. "Why did you do it?" It was an empty question. There was no answer that would have satisfied me.

He was tired of the question, tired of my feelings. He blew up. "I did it because she treated me like shit in high school," he said. "And I wanted to fuck her."

I had already known that was the answer that was coming. I had been that woman too.

* * *

When my husband and I first married, we visited my parents in the summer, and we walked to the Corner Store to get out of the house in the evenings. We strolled down the street, hands entwined, lilac bushes blooming around us. Laundry hung on the line of the river company house next door, tents and kayaks scattered around the yard, river guides lounging in their hammocks. Children rode bikes in the middle of the quiet street. The sun remained high long into evening, before dipping behind the crisp blue and white peaks of the Beaverhead Mountains. We never needed anything at the store. We just wanted to enjoy the sun, the walk, the smell of the Idaho air. My home became his home. No one had ever understood me like him.

When things got bad, I stopped going home in the summer for a while. I didn't want anyone to know me. I had put on weight. The weight didn't accumulate slowly. It was quick. My body was angry—so angry—and it consumed, consumed, consumed. It was as though each cell contained an imprint of his fist, like DNA markers.

The fat didn't protect me. It didn't make it hurt any less.

I thought that, if the people in my hometown saw me, they would see my brokenness. I was no longer the girl who fell in love with boys she never spoke to, who laughed in the yard with her best friend, who trusted a boy so implicitly that she flipped through *Playboy*s with him and didn't think he had an agenda, who didn't realize that the boy with the burned-off fingertips was probably, truly dangerous.

They wouldn't like who I had become.

* * *

My experience of being banned from checking out dirty books at the library taught me that libraries were not anonymous, so I started buying self-help books on my e-reader. Books I would have scoffed at earlier. Books with names like *Narcissistic Lovers. The Betrayal Bond*. And later, *The Domestic Violence Recovery Workbook*. I was desperate for answers.

I learned that I was a codependent. I learned that the term was meaningless. I learned that chaos was unusually normal for me. I learned that the stimulation became like an addiction for survivors. I learned that I was addicted to those who were not good for me. I learned that I should have seen the signs. I learned that there were no signs. I learned that it was his fault. I learned that it was my fault. I learned that it was my mother's fault. I learned that it was his mother's fault. I learned that it was society's fault. I learned that I was fine just exactly as I was.

I did not learn how to save my marriage or my husband. The lessons were all pointless.

I was no longer that sharp point in the middle of the compass. Instead, I was the line circling—round and round—and the sharp point was everything that happened to me. I rotated helplessly. This is my life. This is yours. This is yours. This is yours. This is yours. This is yours.

The cashier slapped the pack of Pall Malls on the counter. She typed the numbers into the register. "Where's the horse?" asked the woman in line.

The cashier looked surprised. "What?"

"The horse. Where's the horse that did that to you?"

It was obviously a challenge. The line grew longer behind me. Everyone but me looked away. No one believed a horse had done that to her. The woman in front of me waited for an answer. "In the pasture," said the cashier. "Are you going to pay or not?"

The woman in line turned to her teenage son. "Give me the card," she said. He handed her a credit card but told her it didn't have any money available on it. She handed it to the cashier anyway. The woman's card was declined. "Run it again," she said.

I stared at the bruise on the cashier's face, unable to look away. My heart sped up, head light. Megan, now a counselor, is still my best friend. "When this happens," she says, "you need to take a deep breath. You need to tell yourself that you are safe. You are not there anymore."

I took a deep breath, trying to conceal that I was on the verge of hyperventilation. I didn't want my beer anymore. I wanted to put it back, but that would seem rude. *I am safe*, I told myself. *I am safe.*

My heart slowed. I believed it.

I was safe.

She might not have been, but I was.

The cashier looked back at the woman in line, then slid the card across the counter. "Nope," she said. The woman in line stood there.

"Ma'am," I said. "I can pay for it." Both of the women looked at me, surprised. "Really, I don't mind at all."

I put my beer on the counter and took out some cash. I handed the woman in line the cigarettes and oranges. She shrugged her shoulders. "Alright," she said. She turned and left. I turned back to the cashier to pay.

"You didn't have to do that," she said. "She pulls that shit all the time."

"It's okay," I said. "I've been there." I caught myself staring at the bruise again. She saw me, her hand rising back to her face, her expression softening.

"Well, that was real nice of you anyway," she said.

The night before, I had seen Pete for the first time in years. I hugged him so hard. He had married a woman with wide eyes and a kind face. His wife and I both had red hair, the same graduate degree, and we happened to be wearing the same earrings. "I like you," I said. We all laughed. Pete and I told stories, still easy with each other after so many years. He teased me because I hadn't known where the hymen was. I teased him about asking Megan for permission to kiss him.

"I think that's sweet," his wife said. "That he asked for permission."

I thought about what she said. It *had* been sweet, I realized. How wrong it was of me to ever think that asking for permission was anything less.

You're right to think about leaving.

You Are the Star

When I was in an undergraduate creative writing workshop, the professor was an artist in addition to being a writer. At the end of the semester, she painted each of us a little card with watercolors and a French word. She said she had meditated and chosen the word that suited us as individuals the most. She handed out the cards and told each student what their word meant. When she handed me my card, she said nothing.

I looked at it, and on it was written "étoile." I had studied French, but I didn't recognize this word. *What does it mean?* I asked.

She looked around at the other students. *You know what it means*, she said.

No, I don't, I said.

She leaned in and whispered, *It means star. You are the star.*

Stars can burn for a long time, but they eventually die. The heat is what makes us see the star in the sky, but also, what eventually kills it.

✻ ✻ ✻

When I was born on Christmas Day many years ago, the stars in the sky were at such an alignment that my astrological chart has more of the element fire than any other element. I have too much fire. I feel everything intensely, and I react to everything intensely. The astrologer who showed me this in a reading said that my challenge in life is to stop burning so hot.

My friend Rebecca tells me, *When I think of you, the word "bright" comes to mind. Your eyes, voice, and colors. You're a bright spot to me.*

I tell Rebecca, *When I think of you, the word "light" comes to mind.* Rebecca's *light* is the kind of light that I want to climb into. I want to nap inside of it like a cat in sunlight. I want it wrapped around me.

My *bright* is the kind that consumes.

My ex-husband used to say, *You excite me. No one has ever excited me like you.*

A woman writes me and says, *You are the fiercest, most independent woman I know.*

A close friend says to me, *I can understand why some people question the abuse, only because when I met you, I couldn't imagine something like that happening to someone so strong.*

My father said to me after I left my ex-husband, *I just don't know what to believe. You have always been a person who seemed like everything was going fine, until it wasn't.*

My mother said to me when I was in high school, *It never seemed like you needed our help. Your brother always asked for it. But you? It's like you went into your room at eleven and never came out. You always wanted to do everything on your own terms.*

I wanted to say to my mother, *But I needed your help. I needed it.* To my mother, my fire made me appear strong, but she didn't know how truly tender I was.

I asked my ex-husband for help. Begged. There were times when I begged on my knees for his forgiveness because I thought I had deserved what he had given me. There were times when I sat against the bathroom door with my feet propped against the counter to give me leverage, as he slammed against the door rhythmically. *Slam. Slam. Slam.* I begged him to stop.

Some days, I wonder if that door is still cracked open from where he banged against it. Some days, I wonder if there are still holes in the wall above the bed from where he threw the bed knobs at me while I shook under the sheets. Some days, I wonder if his new girlfriend sees those holes and those cracks. Some days, I wonder what stories he tells her to explain those things.

Before I moved out of that house, I took pictures of all of the damage. I keep those pictures locked up with everything else I have locked up. Some days, I wonder how it would feel to *set fire to it all*? In the end, I begged him to leave me. I begged him to leave me because it was so hard for me to leave him. I never wanted to be a beggar.

After my divorce, Rebecca, who was my biggest support system in the immediate aftermath of the abuse, wrote about me, "That strong, independent woman was always her, and he took that away for some time. What's real in us stays, even when we have to work to get back in touch with it."

Some days, I am tired of being strong. I am tired of burning so hot, but I know it was my heat that saved me.

I can never say this enough: Strong women get abused. Sometimes, our strength just means we're able to take it more, and harder, and for longer.

On the day that professor gave me the card that said *star*, I was not the star of my own life. I was being abused. I was wounded, but she couldn't see that because I was also the girl who *went into her room at age eleven and never came out*. I was also the girl for whom *everything was going fine, until it wasn't*. I was also the woman who later heard in the hallway from another creative writing professor, *You are always so happy in person, but your writing is so sad.*

Leslie Jamison writes that wounds are different than damage. Wounds can have a certain beauty to them, but damage is irreparable. When I read those words, I wonder, *Am I wounded, or am I damaged?*

My ex-husband loved my fire; it excited him, but he wanted to control it. In *Trauma and Recovery*, Judith Herman writes, "A single traumatic event can occur almost anywhere. Prolonged, repeated trauma, by contrast, occurs only in circumstances of captivity." My ex-husband knew this intuitively. He wanted my fire to serve him. To achieve that, he had to keep me captive because fire doesn't like to serve.

Some days, I wonder whether, if I hadn't had so much fire, he would have hurt me in the ways that he did. Then, I have to remind myself it doesn't matter. He wasn't allowed to try and break me. He wasn't allowed to love me in ways that wanted me broken.

There was no room for any *star* in our household but him.

My ex-husband gets to sleep under those holes in the wall now. He was the one who put the holes in the wall, and he is the one who gets to sleep under them. Still, I am the one living with the damage. Some days, I think my fire is what saved me, and some days, I think my fire is what put me in harm's way. Other days, I think that those of us who carry darkness inside need the fire to illuminate all that still sparkles. The fire is the star.

The Sun Is at the Beginning of the House

It was the Christmas Eve candlelit service, and I had the honor of lighting the candles. In addition to the two candles on the altar, there were five advent candles in a wreath, and as I lowered the flame to the first advent candle, it blew out. I stopped. Looked back at my father, the usher. Everyone was staring at me expectantly. I was only eight years old. My hands shook. My father walked down the aisle, put his hands around mine. Steadied them. Together, we lit the remaining candles. The shadows made patterns on the ceiling, and during the service, I saw flowers. My imagination danced with them. *I made that*, I thought. It was magic.

The most secure I've ever felt in myself and my world was in the weeks just after summer church camp in the seventh grade. I'd spent a week in the woods, where we'd played games, canoed, painted, and had nightly gospel service. On the final night of camp, the counselors put on a play—a reenactment of Jesus's crucifixion. I was captivated. Every hair on my body stood on end. As Jesus called out to his father, "My God, my God, why have you forsaken me?" I wept. When he said, "Father, forgive them, for they know not what they do," I quieted. Who was I, a lowly sinner, to deserve all of this grace? I believed in God's pure love for me, in his absolute forgiveness.

I went home and told my parents that I was only listening to Christian music from then on. My mom said, "We're not really those kinds of Christians," and she was right. I lost interest in the Christian music after about a week. It would be longer before I lost interest in religion, but that happened too.

When I was twelve, the theme during my confirmation lessons was "God's Plan." Every Wednesday, I would take the school bus down a country highway to the tiny wooden church where the pastor would tell us about God's plan for us. *God had a plan for everyone, you see?* It was all predetermined. But also, we had free will. "How can both of those things be true?" I asked the pastor. "If there is already a plan in place for me, then I can't really have free will, can I?"

"You need to have faith," he said.

"What is faith?" I asked.

"Faith," he said, "is when you trust and believe in God, even when there is no proof."

I lay on my bed with my best friend, the lights out. Candles flickered around us. We were listening to the Cure's *Disintegration*. Outside, the Idaho snow was cold and hard, but in this room, everything was warm. The edges foggy. We were sixteen, and I had an impulse to kiss my friend, but I didn't. I had never kissed anyone. My bedroom had a popcorn ceiling with gold specks throughout. We watched the patterns from the candles dance through the sparkles. Something like a sob rose up in my chest, and I started to weep. "What's wrong?" my friend asked. I told her, *I don't know.* She reached over, took my hand, and we watched the solar system unfold above us.

At church, the pastor's sermon was about how homosexuality was a sin. A woman sat in the front row. She lived with my school librarian—"her friend." Everyone knew they were more than friends. This woman in the front row was devout. She came to church every Sunday, but my school librarian did not.

I was in the eleventh grade and the editor in chief of the school newspaper. I'd recently written an editorial about how we shouldn't strip queer (though we didn't use that word back then) populations of their rights. I'd written this editorial in response to Idaho's Proposition 1, which was a bill that sought to restrict the rights of anyone who wasn't heterosexual. My editorial had been part of a "Point/Counterpoint" series. A guy named Steve wrote the counterpoint. I don't remember his arguments, only that he finished with the sentences "God made Adam and Eve. Not Adam and Steve." Years later, I would see Steve in Boise, where we'd both gone to college. He was almost always accompanied by his best friend, who was gay. I said nothing.

After the editorial was published, the school librarian took me aside and quietly thanked me. A week later, the pastor gave his sermon. The woman in the front row must have surely felt targeted. I felt targeted too. And that was it. The end. That was when I lost my religion.

✳ ✳ ✳

My son was in bed, and I was in my writing loft. Newly divorced, I still struggled with the solitude. I lit a candle. Opened the window. Below me, frogs belched. Crickets buzzed in a singular note that rose, surfaced, then dipped down again. It was a kind of music. I was trying to untangle the ways in which the God of my childhood had both comforted and terrorized me. Thinking of how, when my ex-husband had admitted to his physical abuse of me, my former mother-in-law told him to "put your cares at the foot of the cross." Thinking of how I had envisioned myself splayed upon that cross. Thinking of how my own father had told me that he didn't believe me.

I heard the words "Father, why have you forsaken me?" in my heart, like a deep cry. I looked into the candle flame, and its warmth drew me in, comforted me. I was not going to die for anyone's forgiveness.

I was at a picnic table at Ghost Ranch in New Mexico, where Georgia O'Keeffe had famously painted landscapes. It was clear why she had chosen this place. The brilliant pink cliffs. The expansive blue sky.

A fire burned nearby, and I was surrounded by women. We were there for a writer's retreat. My stay had been paid for by a fellowship. I could have never afforded it on my own. This was the last night of the retreat, and we had read from our work, drank wine, and danced together before collapsing next to the fire.

Earlier in the evening, I'd stood in the middle of a labyrinth and prayed that God would bring me some comfort, some healing. My divorce had been so hard on me. I had very little money, and I was raising my child alone while completing a PhD program. I was lonelier than I'd ever been. I wanted—no *needed*—some hope. I didn't believe in God by then, but I was desperate.

Was it a prayer? Or a plea? Or a cry? Maybe a little bit of each.

Something flew by my ear. It was probably a bat, but I told myself it was a fairy. The magical environment of Ghost Ranch was rubbing off on me. It was a comfort.

Later, at the fire, a woman drew a tarot card for me: the Lovers. The characters entwined on the card look like Adam and Eve in the Garden of Eden. The tarot card reader told me not to fear love. *I won't fear love*, I told myself.

The next morning, when I left my casita, there was a beautiful, intact, and sparkling piece of shale in front of the door. I looked to see where it could have come from, but there was no shale to be found in the hills nearby. Someone or something must have put it there for me. It sits beside me as I write now.

The power was out, so my lover and I lit candles. It was the middle of winter—a cold snap—but my apartment was still warm. My son was at his dad's house. My lover laid a blanket down on the floor, and we spread tarot cards for the new year before having the most intense sex of my life. I call him my *lover* because, at the time, he was more than a friend but less than a boyfriend. There are so few words for this particular kind of intimacy. We embraced on the ground as candlelight sparkled around us. I prayed—not to God this time but to Spirit—*Please let this last.*

During the pandemic, I wrote on social media that I was sad. So very sad. Perhaps I was performing my pain, as Leslie Jamison would say, but I was lonely and wanted to be witnessed to. A woman messaged me and said that she had read my memoir. She was a therapist, but also an intuitive. Her clients sometimes felt the benefits of multiple therapy sessions in one with her. She offered to speak with me for free if I needed it, and I was desperate. *Why not?* When I first saw her face on the computer screen—her open, expressive eyes and big smile—I knew she was going to help me, and she did. She taught me how to communicate to my lover what I needed in a way that he could hear. She told me *not to fear love.* She was magic.

The internet told me the spring equinox was a good time for setting intentions, and I was not in a happy place in my life. I wrote on a small piece of paper, "Truly equal and reciprocal love." And then, "Book." I wanted more commitment from my lover than he was giving me, and though I had already published my first book, I was finding it difficult to finish and send out my second book. I felt as though life was moving on, but I was not keeping up. I folded the paper into a square, placed it under a candle, and lit the flame.

With the psychic therapist's help, I am married now—to my lover—and I am finishing my second book.

What are prayers if not wishes cast into the universe?

* * *

Linda from my hometown, a survivor herself who had found my work meaningful, handwove a shawl for me on a loom. The shawl was based on my astrological chart. She sent a letter with it. The ending read:

> *When a celestial body appears in a house, it affects the entire house. You will be able to see blue-violet threads radiating to the right of Saturn itself. This is because the position of the planet is at the beginning of the house. The blue of Sagittarius is hardly visible as the influences of the three planets are appearing throughout. The sun is at the beginning of the house, so the yellow radiates to the right. The quiet area where only two colors show represents the constellations and houses. The whole work represents my esteem for you.*
>
> *Much love,*
> *Linda*

To this day, I have never been gifted something that is more meaningful to me. I know there is magic woven into that shawl. She sent it at a time when I needed some.

Two years later, when I was thinking of breaking up with the man who would later be my husband, she wrote me a letter where she gently advised against letting someone so tender and kind go. She described meeting her second husband. He was also a sometimes inscrutable but tender and kind man. They had been happily married for years. I would not have listened to anyone else, but there was something about Linda. Quiet and wise and rooted entirely in love. *I won't fear love*, I told myself.

I took the man who would later be my husband to my hometown for the first time. I had promised that we would visit Linda. We walked up the dry, hot road from my parents' house to Linda's. She was housebound because her husband was in a wheelchair and needed round-the-clock care. When we knocked on the door, she squealed with delight and welcomed us in. Hugged me so tightly. Her silver hair in long double braids. Her husband wheeled over to say hello, but I'm not sure he remembered me. Linda's son, who I had gone to high school with, was also there. He and I hadn't known each other well, and he seemed bemused by my appearance but was so loving toward his mother. We went into the kitchen, where she pulled cookies out of the oven.

She showed me a project she was working on in the yard. Multiple clotheslines filled with colorful origami birds that floated in the wind. She had made them to help grieve the loss of her sister. They had started the project together, but Linda had finished it on her own. Because the birds were paper, they would eventually dissolve in the wind and elements.

We ate cookies, and at one point, she hugged me again, with tears in her eyes, and she told me how much I'd meant to her. I was speaking out about the things she couldn't. Her first husband, a Mormon, had been much older, and the Mormon community was clannish and patriarchal. Silence was valued more than truth. She must have felt so alone. She must have felt so many screams breaking inside of her.

I was certainly not the first person to write about abuse, but I was someone who had hung out with her kids and been in her home. There is an intimacy in sharing an experience with someone you've known for a long time. I already knew that she had been magic for me, but seeing the way she looked at me, I realized I had been magic for her too. Sometimes the world gives you what you need, whether you know you need it or not.

My husband and I married in our living room. It was an exceedingly casual ceremony. Our friends crowded on the couch or stood. My son wore shorts and socks. We had no decorations, except for a floral wreath we'd strung above the French doors under which we married. Still, I turned a speaker into a kind of altar. I laid Linda's shawl over it, then gently placed my piece of shale onto the shawl. I lit a candle, and we said our vows. It was one of the most magical moments of my life.

I am not a true practitioner of magic, witchcraft, or even woo-woo. I am a dabbler, and I do not follow any kind of tradition. To my knowledge, I have no magical people in my lineage, though my paternal grandmother very obviously had some intuitive qualities. My mother was an orphan, so I don't even know who my ancestors are on that side. All of this is to say that I have no expertise on the subject of magic. Only a kind of trust and hope. Almost every magical thing I have ever done has stemmed from desperation, from a feeling that the world or the people around me could not give me what I needed. I do not claim to know much about paganism or witchy beliefs or ancestry work, and I try to be respectful, to be honest about how little I know. Like a lot of people, I lost my faith in a patriarchal sky god, and I sought to fill that absence in other ways. I don't believe in manifestation. I don't believe in demons. There is a lot I don't believe in, but I believe in prayer. No, I have *faith* in prayer because I believe in it even though I have no proof. What if the magic is in the willingness to dream? What are prayers if not wishes cast into the universe?

When the man who would become my husband and I left Linda's house, I stopped for a moment to look at those beautiful birds floating on strings. It was a hot Idaho summer. The grass parched and brown. The sky was blue and cloudless, and those colorful birds danced in it. Linda was a true artist. An alchemist. She had made this beauty out of nothing but paper and string. As I gazed at the magic she'd brought into this little piece of the world—my little piece of the world—I realized that everyone and everything eventually dissolve into nothingness, but there is so much beauty in the dance before the dissolution, and that's the point, isn't it?

PART 2

RUPTURE

Whirling Disease

Before:

We piled into a car, four girl-women in our early twenties, a tent, a cooler full of food, and a plastic baggie full of magic mushrooms. The car wound along the tight curves of the river, canyon walls rising sharply on either side, sunlight filtering through the glass.

We stood in the middle of a stream, skirts tucked up around our waists, passing a fly rod between us and casting a line. The line flicked forward, hesitated gracefully in an arc before landing softly on the water. The cold stream funneled around us. We broke the arc of that glassy water. A silver glitter danced by my feet. A trout. It broke the surface, creating a circle, radiating into more circles, then slipping away soundlessly.

We stood on a mountain; the valley stretched below us. More mountains in the distance. The winding stream now just a thin black line. We took photos of each other. Our hair blew in the wind while we leaned forward. Blue Idaho sky stretched endlessly behind us.

We arrived at the hot springs, a large, deep pool shimmering at the base of one of those mountains. We set up our tent. We ate our mushrooms, stuffing down the chalky, earthy harshness. We went for a hike to the place my friend called the "womb of mother earth." We bushwhacked through greenery—no trail in sight—how had she found this magical place? We stood under a jagged white rock that formed a cave around us. We reached out and touched each other's faces, the light softening the edges of our fingers.

We found the "womb." We giggled. My friend told me to press my face to a rock and let the water run over me like the slick back of an otter. I pressed my face to the mossy rock. The warm water formed a pocket around me. I breathed in steam while the water rushed over my head. I opened my eyes. The rock teemed with life. I gasped. Bugs crawled over each other. A white, bulbous spider munched on a fly. I wasn't afraid, but I shivered.

Steam filled my lungs, the heat expanding in the red inside me. I pulled away gasping. We giggled our way back to the spring, the sky darkening around us. There were other people there: a couple from Vienna and a pilot named Bob from Wisconsin. We shed our clothing on the way to the water, leaving a trail behind us. Even my modest friend timidly took off her shirt. We slipped into the warm water, floating on our arms. The man from Vienna danced around the spring playing his harmonica. He, too, was naked.

Bob said, "Why the hell not?" and off came his suit.

The sky opened up above me, stars stretching into another silvery veil. I floated on my back. "Isn't it beautiful?" I asked Bob. "It's like a sequined black party gown stretched out above us."

I closed my eyes. The water around me reached up and met the sky. The glittery stars twinkled in the darkness around me. "It's like we're floating in space," I said.

Bob stared at me in wonder. "I want to be where you are," he said.

At least that's what I heard. More likely, he said, "I want to be on what you're on."

In the distance, I heard branches breaking. Men rounded a corner on the trail, silver beer cans in their hands. British tourists who had just gotten off of a river trip.

"Girls!" they shouted, shedding their clothes and running into the water. We smiled and moved over. We made room in that pool.

My first love was a big, beautiful alcoholic who sometimes raged at me when he drank, who sometimes cried in my arms, and who sometimes held me tenderly.

I took him to the hot springs, my special place, a year after that magical night. We spent the entire day there alone, swimming, picnicking, and sunning on towels by the spring. He told me how beautiful my hometown was, how beautiful I was, how much he loved me, how he wanted to spend his life at that pool with me.

He drank too much wine. Or whiskey. I can't remember. Always one or the other.

On the drive back, he pulled over and parked near the place where my friends and I had cast that beautiful fly line into the clear water. We made love in the back of his truck. He was older, more educated, wealthier than me. I had so much to learn from him. I was a good pupil.

When he left me, I stopped eating, stopped sleeping, grew smaller. I wanted to be so small I could disappear. I wanted to hide my head on that slick rock by the hot springs, let the water wrap around me, and return to that magical womb.

After the alcoholic, I loved a fish biologist. We hiked into a clean mountain lake. He cast a fly line into the clear water while I sunned on a rock, reading Edward Abbey. He didn't catch any fish. I came up behind him, wrapped my arms around his waist. I pointed at the water.

"There's one," I said.

He sighed. "That one has whirling disease," he said. "It can't stop spinning. It will eventually spin itself to death."

"That's so sad," I said.

I saw it then. The useless spins. The loss of control.

That night, I awoke in my sleeping bag, and my lover was gone. I unzipped the tent and found him outside, sitting on a flat rock, staring into the distance. I wrapped my legs around his waist, laid my head on his shoulder, and we watched that still water together. A fat moon hung above us. The fish spun hopelessly below us.

After:

I met my husband in a bar. He danced with my best friend. She pulled down his pants as a joke, and he kept dancing in his boxer shorts. He made me laugh.

I wanted to know him better.

Then, the baby came.

The baby split me in two. I screamed at the final moment, as the yellow line on the monitor reached its peak, then my flesh ripped. Relief. The baby slipped onto the table, slick and red. And crying.

Was I crying? I can't remember.

I remember my husband crying. And smiling. The nurse brought the baby to my breast, laid his skin against mine. My husband couldn't stop crying.

My husband later told me that, when he saw the pain I was in, he couldn't stand it. He knew things about himself that I didn't know yet. He wanted to tell me. There was so much he wanted to tell me. He was so, so sorry.

But I didn't know any of this while my baby rooted at my chest. I only knew that feeling. I only knew my husband's eyes, so full of love and hope, and something that also looked like guilt, but I didn't yet know what guilt looked like.

When the baby came, I didn't yet know that my husband would go fishing when his rage overcame him. He would never catch any fish. I would make fun of him for bait fishing when fly fishing seemed so much more elegant. I would make fun of him for never catching any fish.

This would become a joke for us.

But also, I would sob while he was gone. I would wonder if he was coming back. I would wonder if he was even fishing. I would know there had been other women.

* * *

Desperation clawed at my insides. Desperation sliced me open at the gills.

When the baby came, I didn't yet know that, years later, I would call my dad from my computer because my husband had broken my phone in a rage. I would cry, "Dad, he beat me up." My dad wouldn't know what to say. My dad wouldn't know what to do. He lived over three thousand miles away. He didn't know what to do.

When the baby came, I didn't yet know that, on the same day I called my dad from my computer, my husband would get so angry that he would hurl his own phone into a river. And because neither of us had a phone, his mother emailed me a few days later to tell me someone had found his phone in the water. It still worked. I was so angry that his phone still worked. But mine was broken.

When the baby came, I didn't yet know that my husband and I would dance while the baby slept upstairs. I wasn't a very good dancer, and he was worse. We stumbled over each other's feet, but we kept trying.

I remembered dancing with another man before I met my husband. That man spun me with such strength and precision that my footwork felt effortless. We spun in circles, glittery lights above us that looked like stars. We whirled underneath a ceiling that looked like the sky.

* * *

When the baby came, I didn't yet know that I would soon be fighting my own impulse to spin. I didn't yet know what it felt like to be helpless.

The knife slices into the silver gills, exposes the pink meat underneath. Do fish feel pain? Do their shocked eyes look at us and beg us to stop right before the knife pierces their flesh? Or are they simply relieved to have it over with?

I am using the fish as a metaphor because fish are the most useless of animals.

When the baby came, I didn't yet know that my marriage would end with a 911 call. I had a new phone by then.

I didn't yet know I would finally do it. I would dial the final 1 in the sequence of numbers that changed my life.

When the baby came, I didn't yet know that my husband would leave me in handcuffs, but he would want to come home.

I didn't yet know that I would stare at our wedding photo for a long time, wondering what to do. In the photo, I was smiling, hopeful. He looked so young. His eyes were so kind. When that photo was taken, I didn't yet know what his contempt looked like. I only knew his kindness.

I remembered when the fish biologist had given me a framed photo of himself. In the photo, he knelt by a cold, clear river. He held a silver steelhead in his hands. He was smiling. I returned the photo after the relationship ended, but I regretted it. I missed his image.

I remembered another photo of the alcoholic smiling at me from the spring, only his head above the clear water. I kept that photo, tucking it into the back of an old photo album. My husband would not have liked it if he had known.

I knew that the hot spring was gone. A forest fire burnt over it and filled it with ash. It was a different fire from the one that had killed a friend only a few ridgelines away. He was a smoke jumper. He had tried to run, but the fire was too swift. When they found his body, his fire blanket—silver and steely—lay uselessly next to him.

When the baby came, I didn't yet know that my husband would want to come home after the arrest. That I would let him back into my home for two more days. That my husband would not change, but I would.

In the summer, after the baby came, we went to Dagger Falls on the Salmon River where the salmon jump. They are called Dagger Falls because of the sharp black rocks that poke out of the frothy white water. I had once found an arrowhead at Dagger Falls, black obsidian carved into a sharp point. I pocketed it, even though I shouldn't have. I should have left it where I found it. *Take only memories. Leave only footprints.*

I tried to take part of that wilderness home with me, but I lost it.

I thought of that as I stared at those falls. Maybe it had been karma. Maybe I had lost the arrowhead because I never should have tried to take something that didn't belong to me.

I didn't think I deserved to have anything beautiful in my life.

The salmon sprung out of the water. They hit the rocks with loud thwacks. It must have been painful. Some of them found the right route—natural steps built into the falls that they could navigate—but some of them did not. One of them kept flopping back into the water, shocked for a moment, then sprung back up and jumped again. Hit the black rock again. Fell again. And again. And again.

It couldn't help itself. It couldn't change its nature.

"Isn't it beautiful?" I asked my husband. "The persistence?"

"But aren't they just returning to the place of their birth so they can die?" he asked me.

I stared at that fish, fighting for its right to die. "I guess so," I said. I thought of my former lovers, of how much it had hurt when those lovers had left me, of how I hadn't let go of that hurt until I met my husband, of how I'd hoped that when we married, it meant I would never have to hurt like that again. I looked at my husband and felt that we wouldn't be married forever.

I held my chubby baby in my arms. He smiled at me and reached his little hands out to touch my face. The water raged below us, and for a moment, I wanted to jump in.

I smiled at my baby, holding him up above the water, so he too could see the salmon jumping, their silver-and-red bodies glinting like blades. My baby laughed. I held him tightly. I wouldn't let him go. I might jump, but I wouldn't take him. I wouldn't let him be swept into those waves with me.

Poppies

Poppies grow wild in the yard across the street from my childhood home. They crowd the thick grass, choking a tiny log cabin with charred streaks across the wood. The glass in the windows of the cabin is gone, chicken wire in its place. When I walk by, I imagine the sunlight filtering through the chicken wire, casting checkered shadows across the black, burnt floorboards of the cabin. The house burnt down years ago—the owner passed out inside the bright flames.

He had no heirs. No one to step in and clear out the log ruins. No one to sell his creek-side lot. No one to raze the building to the ground, tear out the thick grass and weeds, upturn the soil, pile the debris into a truck, and cultivate a space free of wild poppies.

Poppies are my favorite flower. Fire followers, they germinate in the aftermath of destruction. Once, I walked by his home and wanted so badly to reach out and pluck some for a tableside arrangement, but I couldn't. It was as though the poppies grew directly from the ashes of his body and bones mixing with the soil.

✽ ✽ ✽

I spend the summers living in my childhood home, but during the academic year, I live in a hollow in Appalachia. I once described it to a friend as a *holler*. She asked me what that means, and I didn't know how to explain it: *It's a road that extends back into the woods*, I said. *It's very green and overgrown. People live in clusters. They have lots of stuff in their yards. I'm sorry*, I finished. *That's all bullshit. I don't know how to describe it without sounding classist. It's a beautiful place, but the people seem sad.*

At night, I run in the dark hollow. I wear a headlamp; a white circle bounces in front of me. The dogs howl from top to bottom. In Idaho, the state where I was raised, the howls of hounds echo through the open landscape. Like desolation. In Appalachian Ohio, the howls are muffled. Like despair.

Moon-glowed faces peer out at me from front doors. I keep running, the air, thick, heavy, and misty. The greenery is alive; insect sounds press on me like fingerprints, desperate in their urgency. I think of how the road in the hollow feels like an arm extending into the hillside, of how my house sits at the end, and I am a beating red heart inside that house. I think that, with every house I pass, we are all pulsing along the vein of this road.

I am intimate with loneliness. The loneliness of my twenties has changed now that I am in my thirties. It has less to do with the absence of company and more to do with an awareness that when my eyes close at night and open in the morning, I am always alone.

✶ ✶ ✶

A decade or so ago, when he was still alive, I saw that neighbor sitting on a bar stool at the Owl Club, a dive bar on Main Street. The entire front of the building that houses the bar is a wooden, shingled owl. The owl is a false front, a façade. A false front usually hides cheap construction, but in this case, the false front masks a beautiful nineteenth-century brick building. The Owl is kitsch that masks beauty. Poking out of one of the owl's eyes are two arrows. No one knows where the arrows originated. They poke into the sky, free of history. A professor, a refugee from Eritrea, later told me that the only way to live free of trauma is to live without history, and those words spoke to me. Still, very little in this town is free from history.

This Idaho winter, a winter in my early twenties, was bitter cold. Bodies crowded the warm bar, the air hazy in its heat. I stood next to a young friend, Tim, who wanted to be more than my friend, but I was still in love with an older man who no longer wanted to be my lover.

Most nights, I drove for hours along the winding, icy river dreaming of this older man. I had spent my entire life feeling unwanted until I met him. He was older than me, more educated, passionate, and charismatic. He'd made me feel loved in a way that no one ever had. At the same time, no one else had ever made me feel as low.

I read a poem by Anne Boyer once:

If an animal is shocked, escapably or inescapably,
she will manifest deep attachment for whoever has shocked her.

I knew her words to be true. The spin cycle was addicting. When he left me, desperation set in, and my nightly drives began. I parked, sat by the blue water of the river, and cast incantations into the air, begging the universe to bring him back to me. I burned his letters then regretted it. I drank potions given to me by an herbalist to calm my nerves, then sank into a deep, hot bath, and waited for darkness.

When Tim came to town, it was a distraction from my longing. At the Owl Club that night, his hand grazed my shoulder. I smiled, stepped closer to him.

Before entering the bar, Tim and I had sat in my car in the parking lot, the engine idling, Neil Young's *Harvest Moon* playing on the CD player. I ran my finger along the steam of the window. I drew a wet heart.

"I have something to show you," he said. "I want you to know the truth about me."

He reached up and took off his baseball cap. "I have psoriasis," he said. He lowered his head. It was shaved and patched with red.

"Is that all?" I asked. "Oh Tim, I don't care about that." I reached out and touched his scalp tenderly. His body slumped against mine, resting against my chest. "It's okay," I said, stroking his head. "I like you just the way you are."

His shoulders heaved, tears soaking my shirt. This wasn't the first time his tears had soaked my shirt. We had a history of his longing, his sadness, and my withholding, but this was the first time I accepted his embrace.

I didn't know how not to. He had taken his hat off for me.

After Tim recovered, wiped his eyes, and we entered the bar, just after he stepped closer to me, just after his hand grazed my shoulder, just after I accepted the offering of his body collapsing into my chest, just after I accepted the offering of his shame, just after I let him into my car on a dark winter's night when I knew what he wanted from me, but I also knew I was in love with someone else—in the moment just after all of those things—my neighbor fell off his bar stool. He fell and his head made contact with a table on the way down. He sat dazed on the floor, bleeding. The blood was so fast, so great, so red—bright pink almost—rivulets quickly turning into a stream.

He sat on that floor like a child, and looked up at me, his poppy-red face glistening, eyes so sad.

Everyone scattered. No one would help him. I grabbed Tim's arm, and we rushed over. I kneeled down beside him. Tim asked the bartender for a rag and held the rag to my neighbor's bleeding head. My neighbor looked up, ashamed.

"I have to tell you something," he said, as Tim held that blood-soaked rag. My neighbor closed his eyes, then opened them again. "I have hepatitis."

Tim looked down at his hand on this man's bloody head, but he kept it there. "It's okay, man," he said. "Let's just get you home."

He helped the man up. The bartender shook his head at us. Tim helped the man out to my car, put him in the backseat, and we drove to that little log cabin.

In the main room of the cabin, there was only a wood stove, a chair, and a mattress. We put the man in the chair by the stove, so he could stay warm. The man looked at us for a long time, then said, "Thank you."

What I remember is that stove. That black wood stove. And the chair beside it, the warmest place in the cabin during a dark, cold night. And that small man in an even smaller chair, and how his face was so full of gratitude, and so full of shame, and so, so lonely.

I remember his solitude.

Just before the man I married kissed me for the first time, he took off his hat. Only twenty-four, and he already had early male-pattern baldness. He had started balding at fourteen, such a difficult age. He ran his hand over the smoothness of his scalp, visibly uncomfortable. I couldn't resist, I reached over and glided my hand over his head. I had only met him that night. I smiled at him. He leaned over and kissed me quickly, as though I would change my mind.

I didn't know how not to accept his embrace. Just like Tim, he had taken his hat off for me.

Sometimes, I Skype at night with a friend in Idaho. We became friends when we were twenty. We are now in our thirties. I have a photo of her from when we roomed together. She was in tight jeans and a sequined shirt, captured in mid-movement—dancing—her arms raised, hair wild.

Beautiful.

We wear pajamas during our Skype conversations. Our dogs sit in our laps. They eye each other balefully through the computer screens. We each have a glass of wine.

I raise my glass to her. "You know what the worst part of being in your thirties is?" I ask.

She raises her eyebrows.

"When you realize all of those problems you thought you had left behind in your twenties are still there."

"I'll drink to that," she says, taking a sip of her wine.

Some days, I am just an accumulation of my wounds.

Years after the moment at the bar, after my neighbor sat stunned on the floor and stared up at me—bleeding and red-faced—there was another moment.

A terrible moment.

I was the one on the floor.

It was as though I was watching from the outside. It was as though I could see myself staring up at my husband, bleeding and red-faced. I no longer knew who I was, my poppy-red face glistening, eyes so sad.

Some days, I am the light let in by my wounds.

I was in my early twenties when that man fell off his bar stool. I had dropped out of college and was living in my parents' basement. Tim had returned from a stint on a fishing boat in Alaska, a stint that had wrecked him emotionally and physically. We found a balm for our loneliness in each other.

I left my hometown a short while later. I met the man I married, I moved across the country with him. I had a baby. I finished college. He made me homemade scones in the mornings before I woke and left them on the counter with a note: *Smoothie in the fridge. Have a good day today. I know things are hard, but you're such a good mom and wife. I don't know what I'd do without you. Please give me time. Please forgive me.*

And I forgave. I didn't know what I'd do without him either. We found a balm for our loneliness in each other.

At some point, I turned thirty, but I don't remember my thirtieth birthday. I remember my husband's love, his notes, the way his hand smoothed my hair down at night before he fell asleep with his arm around my shoulders. I remember the way I soothed myself by running my hand along his smooth head. It was the same motion I had done as a toddler when my mother still carried me. I sucked two fingers on one hand, the other hand entangled in her hair. Even then, I never wanted to be far from the person I loved.

I also remember my husband's fists, his rages, his words.

I remember believing what he said to me:

You are crazy. You are a fucking cunt. My life was ruined the day I married you. You are the ugliest woman I've ever dated. You make me this way. You provoke me to abuse you.

I remember also believing what else he said to me:

You are amazing. You are such a wonderful mother and wife. No one has ever excited me like you. Sometimes I wake at night and just look at you. You are so beautiful. You are so smart, so talented, so funny. I am so lucky to have found a woman like you. You are the best thing that has ever happened to me.

I am amazing. I am worthless. I am amazing. I am worthless. I am amazing. I am worthless.

I remember feeling grateful that he loved me even though I was such a horrible person that he felt he needed to hit me.

I remember thinking I couldn't leave him because I was too weak to survive the loneliness that would return in his absence.

I don't remember turning thirty, but I remember thinking later:

This cannot be real.

Now, in my thirties, I have divorced my husband, and again, I return home in the summer. I live in my parents' basement. My neighbor's burnt house reminds me of those years in my twenties, when I didn't know what I wanted, when I didn't know my own power, when I didn't know what was coming.

What else is there to say? All patterns either come to an end or continue.

But now, I live in my parents' basement—not because I have nowhere else to go—but because I miss the light in Idaho.

And when I walk by my neighbor's scorched cabin on my evening strolls, I see the poppies growing wildly in the midst of tall grass. They swarm the cabin. They rest their beauty against the black ash.

Poppies might bloom for years following a fire, but eventually will quit blooming until the next fire comes through. In the forests around my hometown, there are good fires and bad fires. It is sometimes difficult in the beginning to tell the difference.

This is what I have learned: There is always another fire.

✶ ✶ ✶

This is also what I have learned: He was the fire. My older lover was the fire. My ex-husband's fists were the fire. His words were the fire. Tim was the fire. My neighbor was the fire.

But I was a fire too.

There was a man in my hometown in the summer after my divorce. We lived on opposite ends of the country during the school year, but there was a moment before we parted for our separate homes. A moment where I said, "Are we still moving slowly?"

And he gripped my waist, buried his head in my hair, and said, "I don't think so."

We had found a balm for our loneliness.

I am thinking of this man as I run in my dark hollow. I did the same thing after my first love left me. I did the same thing after I hurt Tim. I did the same thing with all of the men in between. And I did the same thing when I left my husband.

I ran.

But this time I am running from neither a man nor my pain. I am running to escape my loneliness. Loneliness is more acute following an absence of it, and this hollow, for all of the life within it, feels so solitary. This hollow has probably never seen a fire.

And as I run along this vein, I think of all of the men who I let into my life because I was afraid of loneliness. I think of the ways I let them hurt me, and of the ways in which I hurt them. When I was still with my husband, I told my counselor I could never leave my husband. "I've never left anyone," I said.

And I hadn't.

But, now, while I'm running, I think of how I did eventually leave my husband. I white-knuckled through the dark nights without calling him. I white-knuckled through the desperation. I white-knuckled through the loneliness, and one day, I awoke, and I didn't read his horoscope after reading my own. It struck me that I no longer missed him.

I think of Tim, and how he's probably fine. He's probably found someone who loves him, and I think of how I cared enough about Tim to regret not loving him for a third of my life, and maybe that's enough. Maybe that regret is the only offering I have to give. Maybe it's time to let that regret go.

I think of my older lover who did eventually want me back. I think of the messages I continued to receive from him throughout the years, and of how I finally said, *no more*, because I was no longer willing to go through that spin cycle with him.

I think of this other man, and how we sat on a deck in the Idaho sunlight—two divorced adults—and we had an adult conversation about where our relationship was headed, and we were both honest, and we both felt safe, and in the end, we each placed our individual needs first.

I am thinking of all of this as I run in that dark hollow. Greenery consumes the hillside, the abandoned furniture, the abandoned homes, and the abandoned cars. My loneliness often consumes me in the same way, but it doesn't consume me whole. I white-knuckle through it, and as with those nights after I left my husband, I wake up fine.

It turns out I haven't brought all of my problems from my twenties with me into my thirties.

What else is there to say? Patterns either end or continue.

I am not only an accumulation of my wounds. I am not that greenery from which the landscape can't escape. I am not those abandoned homesteads being swallowed up whole. Most mornings, I wake up grateful for the quiet, for the calm, and for my solitude. The darkness still comes at night, but the mornings are full of light. I will never be that arrow, free of history, but I am also not a circle. I am the beating red heart at the end of the vein. I am the fire. I am the poppies.

▇▇▇ I tell you ▇▇▇▇▇▇▇
▇▇▇▇▇▇▇▇▇▇▇▇▇
▇ these are my real feelings for you.

No, You

It's Friday night—date night—and I'm sitting in a fine dining restaurant in Columbus, Ohio. Candlelight flickers from the table, illuminating the cocktail in front of me. I stare out the window into the shadowy streetscape. A young woman in short denim cutoffs runs across the street, stops, then turns to stare at the young man running after her. She laughs. When he reaches her, she wraps her arms around him, then tips to the side. He holds her up. She laughs harder. She is drunk.

She pulls him toward the bar near them. The bouncer looks on stoically. The young man pulls her arm as if to say, *Come back. Come back.*

She grabs his hand—tugs—as if to say, *No, you. No, you.*

I lean in closer to the glass. *Who will win?*

I hear a noise, look away from the window. The server puts down my roasted cauliflower, cashew, and crispy chickpea soup.

"Are you alone?" he asks.

"Yes."

He smiles at me sympathetically, but I look back out the window just in time to see the young man being pulled into the bright bar by a force he cannot control.

* * *

I don't live in Columbus, Ohio. I live an hour and a half away in the town where I am finishing my PhD, but I'm flying out in the morning to Vermont, where I will spend two weeks at a writer's residency. I'm spending the night at the same hotel that I always stay at—a Days Inn that allows me to park my car for free. In the elevator, there is a poster of a bearded man in a bright blue suit. The first time that I saw that poster, I texted my friend P. J., "I have found your doppelganger at a hotel."

He texted back, "Are you staying at a Days Inn?"

Apparently, I wasn't the first person to have made that connection.

I met P. J. at a bar in my hometown. It was the day after Christmas, and also the day after my thirty-eighth birthday. P. J. was thirty-one, a wildlands firefighter. I mistook him for a different thirty-year-old firefighter whom I had flirted with the summer before. P. J. laughed at me and told me I was wrong. I should have been embarrassed, but I wasn't.

He asked if he could buy me a drink, and I said that he could. He friended me on Facebook the next day and suggested that we go to the hot springs. In my hometown, in rural Idaho, going to the hot springs is "Netflix and chill."

We went to the hot springs.

Only a few winters before, I had spent the day after Christmas curled up in bed and crying in my parents' basement because I had just left my abusive husband who I was still in love with.

Do you know how hard it is to leave someone you still love?

* * *

Still, I had no choice. I could use love to rationalize sacrificing myself to the abuse, but I could no longer rationalize sacrificing my seven-year-old. His father's love wasn't worth the chaos, so I did it. I packed up and moved to another state to get my PhD. I took our seven-year-old son with me, and together, we moved into a tiny apartment on the top floor of a complex that typically houses undergraduates. Our apartment had a galley kitchen with no dishwasher, and we didn't have a washing machine or dryer.

If we were resourceful, we could go for almost a month without washing our clothes, but then I had to pack up all of the laundry, along with the kiddo, and go to the laundromat on the corner where, for hours, we sat side by side while the clothes swished back and forth in the washing machines, and I looked at my little boy—his feet not touching the ground, his nose in a Harry Potter book—and thought, *This was not the childhood I planned on giving him.*

Time in the laundromat felt so long—stretched into painful increments—but it wasn't as long as the nights, especially the nights when my son was at his dad's. Every other weekend, I drove over the state line to the Ritchie County 7-Eleven in West Virginia where my ex-husband and I handed off our son for the one and a half days remaining in the weekend. My ex-husband wasn't abusive to our son, not physically at least, but it was still hard for me to send them off together. I missed my child and worried about him. I missed being a family with my ex-husband too, and seeing him every other weekend reminded me of the dreams we'd had. The Ritchie

County 7-Eleven was in the heart of fracking country, and when I drove back to my tiny apartment, I could see caravans of gas tankers driving past me, flashers twinkling.

I could almost convince myself that they were fireflies.

Once home in my little apartment, what could I do? I knew what I would have done on a weekend when I was married. Together, my husband and I would have cooked an elaborate meal. We called those "date nights." We made bouillabaisse, spaghetti carbonara, chicken with forty cloves of garlic, lamb chops with olive butter.

We ate and loved so well.

But when we weren't eating and loving well, we were fighting. And when we weren't fighting, he was apologizing for whatever way that he had hurt me. There were so many ways. The physical abuse. The insults. The damage to the house. The projection and blame. Scaring the dogs. Scaring our son. Scaring me.

He had so much to apologize for, and he apologized through food. He knew how much I loved food, and how much I loved the time that we spent together preparing it, but soon, when he was beating me most of the time, he was also cooking most of the time. He would hurt me, then prepare me the most elaborate meals that he had ever prepared. He would cook whatever I wanted and I would lap the salty goodness into my bruised mouth.

For a moment, I would feel satiated.

In my marriage, food was love.

And control.

And coercion.

And apologies.

By the end of the marriage, I was rarely cooking. Or driving. Or doing anything that a normal adult would do. I was merely trying to survive.

During the first year in my PhD program, I had to relearn all of those things. I drove my son to school every morning; then home, where I would catch up on reading; then to campus for my classes; then to pick my son up from school; then to the grocery store; then back to the apartment, where I would make dinner—something easy—then put my son to sleep. Finally, after all of that, I would almost always have a good cry before settling in for a late night of writing or homework. It was lonely, exhausting, and terrifying, but I quickly learned that I was more capable than I'd realized, and that knowledge made me want to learn how to love the things I'd once loved again.

Finally, one quiet night, when my son was at his father's, I pulled out a cookbook and chose some recipes my ex-husband would never have wanted to eat. I went to my galley kitchen and started cooking. I baked the beets, then peeled the oranges for a beet, orange, and black olive salad. I made toasted, herbed rice, and I prepared a seasoned yogurt sauce.

Because cooking by myself was boring, I brought my laptop in and set it up in the corner. I streamed *Pretty Little Liars* even though I was twenty years out of that show's demographic. I didn't care. I had no husband in my ear to criticize me for my pedestrian tastes.

Hulu only had the five most recent episodes, so I had no idea what was happening in the story . . .

Who was A?

I mean, Mona is obviously A, right?

That teacher is superhot, but I'm pretty sure it's not okay for him to date a high school student.

Wait, why are they stuck in a house surrounded by creepy dolls?

And then my food was ready. I took a scoop of the rice, placed the beet salad carefully upon it, and added a dollop of yogurt on the side. It was so beautiful that I took a picture and posted it on Facebook.

Then, I poured a glass of wine, sat on my couch, watched more *Pretty Little Liars*, and ate a meal that went down easily after so many others had not. The meal sustained me. I knew that I was safe. I felt satiated.

I had done it all on my own.

This is not where I say I was fixed. I still had so much pain. But I kept getting up in the mornings. Kept driving. Kept doing laundry. Kept cooking for myself.

One night, I cooked spaghetti carbonara for a friend even though the memory of my ex-husband throwing a hot bowl of carbonara on the floor still made me shiver. My friend and I ate the carbonara while watching *Dirty Dancing*, and when I think of carbonara now, I think of my friend.

Another night, I cooked eggplant parmesan for a man who wanted to step in, to do it for me, and I said to him firmly, *I can do this on my own.*

Another night, I made myself cheese and crackers for dinner and wept because single parenting, and graduate school, and my unknowable future were all so overwhelming.

And another night, I walked through the snowy streets of my hometown to P. J.'s house after we had gone to the hot springs, and I didn't feel guilty because the years following my divorce had been long and lonely, and I deserved to have a fling with someone who wasn't going to hurt me.

He told me recently, "You never seemed desperate to me."

I needed to hear that because it's not easy to be alone. It's not easy to be alone five years after my divorce when my ex-husband is already remarried and has another child. It's not easy to be alone when I'm nearing forty and know the world is not kind to women of a certain age. It's not easy to be alone when I'm eating cheese and crackers on the couch.

But in the years since I started my PhD program, I've discovered a version of myself that I never could have been within the context of my marriage. I'm more independent, more creative, and a better mother. I've sold a book to a major publisher. I've made friends with people who excite me and make me laugh. I've traveled to foreign places and had that travel paid for by my work. I've read my writing in bookstores in Manhattan with famous writers. I've learned that I'm not just capable but talented.

I've discovered a world that is so different, and so much better for me, than the world in West Virginia was ever going to be. So when I'm sitting in a fine dining restaurant by myself because I have been fortunate enough to get a fellowship to a writer's residency, and the server sets my soup in front of me just as I'm engrossed in the story of a couple I'll never know, and I take a bite of that soup, which is so creamy, silky, and delicious that it is almost sensual, then I know that I have created the life for myself that I always wanted. I know that the woman I am now was always holding the hand of the woman I was then.

She was always tugging and saying, *No, you. No, you.*

Spoons

"Is it hard?" I asked my childhood friend. I couldn't remember his name—the name of the baby she'd lost. I hadn't been close to her in years. I lived across the country but returned to my hometown to work as a river ranger for the US Forest Service while I was on summer break from my PhD program. My friend's arrival at the wilderness guard station where I worked had been a surprise, but the salmon were running. Her husband wanted to fish, and fishermen had been my only companions for a week.

The last time I saw her was the year before in the grocery store. She hugged me then, her body thin and hard. My eyes connected with her husband's. Startled. For the first time, she wasn't beautiful. Her shoulders jutted out in hard angles. Her face gaunt. Her hair thin with split ends.

My friend had been a stunner her entire life—a rodeo queen with thick black hair and big green eyes who knew how to dress and use makeup to her advantage. She was charismatic too. When she smiled, her smile was so wide, white, and sparkling that it drew people in, magnetized them. Everyone who met her, including me, fell in love with her.

Once, when I was twenty, I'd sat in a restaurant with my friend and an older woman who I didn't know well. My friend was talking to someone at a table nearby, and as I gazed at them, the woman asked me what I was thinking. I was honest. I admitted that I wished people saw me like they saw my friend, that I felt invisible next to her. The woman said to me, not unkindly but also not kindly, "You have to understand that some people have natural advantages when it comes to how they look. You do not have those advantages." She seemed just a little bit mean in that moment, but maybe that's my imagination. I truly have no idea whether she was trying to be helpful or hurtful. Either way, I knew what she meant. I was not, and would never be, a beauty like my friend.

In the grocery store, fifteen years later, as I hugged my friend, her smile was just as wide and sparkling, but there was something frightening in it, and in her eyes too. I was at the store with a co-worker, and as we walked away, we gossiped like two people in a small town. "Did you see how she looked? She looked scary." We rounded a corner, and I stopped in my tracks when I saw the husband staring at me. He didn't even look angry. Just hurt. I said hello to him and pretended like he hadn't heard me, but I never stopped feeling shame.

A year later, my friend and I sat at the picnic table outside of my A-frame. She looked like she was eating. Like she was sober. I held her newborn daughter.

"Sometimes it's hard," she said. "From the side, she looks just like him. The other day, I laid on the floor of her nursery and cried."

"I'm so sorry," I said.

Her eyes shined. "The nurses did compressions on him for so long that they left a divot in his chest. They were crying. They said, 'Don't die, baby,' but he was already dead."

I looked down. I stroked her baby's soft head. "Your daughter is beautiful."

She spoke again. "I keep thinking that one day I'll wake up and have forgiven myself."

I didn't know what to say, didn't know all that had happened during those years when she had struggled with addiction, when she had been thin and hard, when one of her babies had died, when I, too, had been hard, when I had lived across the country with a violent man and a son who could hear my screams from the other room.

When my friend and I were girls, we slept in her bed surrounded by stuffed animals. She spooned me. Held my hand. Our friendship was a love story as much as it was platonic. We were never sexual, but there was real love there. I was captivated by her to the point that my other friends grew angry at me for disappearing. I only wanted to be around this *one*. We drove in her car all night, smoked joints, and shared secrets. I felt as though I could tell her everything. I felt as though her heart was in my own body. Sometimes, after a long night, we stood by the river and watched the sun come up over the mountains. They were the most magical sunrises I've ever seen.

I was a virgin who had never even made out with anyone, and my friend was the opposite. My parents were nice people. Religious people. But my mother and I butted heads. There was a lot of screaming, and at times, my mother was physical. My father, a gentle man, stayed quiet, only intervening with my mother during the most extreme moments. I felt unloved. Abused. In contrast, my friend's parents were secular. They were fun. They lavished love and money and praise onto her. Still, I once saw her father, a professional hunter, beat one of his dogs, who was chained to a pole, with a tire iron.

People couldn't understand why we were friends, and I'm not sure that I understood either. We decided to go to college together, and it was there that our friendship unraveled. We were not enough alike. I wasn't enough of a partier, and she wasn't enough of a student. There was no dramatic finale to the friendship. She dropped out of school, eventually moved back to our hometown, and my life went on without her. I would hear stories about her drug use throughout the years, but I never witnessed it, so until that day in the grocery store, it didn't feel real, and then, at that picnic table a year later, I could only see her as the girl she had been.

What did she see in me? I wondered.

After she left, I sat by myself. Night arrived slowly, the darkness unmarred by electricity. A single light flickered across the river, a golden glow from the lone cabin nearby. I pretended that the light was for us, my friend and me. I felt that it spoke from the darkness. I felt that it said, *You are not alone.* I felt that it said, *You are forgiven.*

I wanted so badly to be forgiven. Forgiven for being unkind to my friend in the grocery store. Forgiven for being jealous of her all those years ago. Forgiven for thinking I was better than her because I'd finished college.

I wanted her to be forgiven for her addiction, for her son's death, for everything that had brought her to that place. Most of all, I wanted her to forgive herself like she craved.

A few years later, her husband died by suicide. According to the small-town gossip, she'd sent one of her children out to their RV to tell him that dinner was ready, and the child had found him. My mother said she'd heard he'd been sober for a few months before that. I don't know how that might have connected to his choice, and I couldn't possibly, but of course I speculated.

On social media, my friend appeared to be doing well. Always happy in her photos. That big, beautiful smile was ever present. She didn't look like the woman I'd seen in the grocery store, and I wondered if she'd alchemized the loss of her husband somehow. Into a life with more stability. More sobriety.

But a few years after that, a different friend texted me that my childhood friend had been arrested for drug possession and sexual abuse of a minor under sixteen. In a small town like mine, it can be so hard to separate the gossip from the truth, but the gossip was that my childhood friend had been hosting minor girls in her home in exchange for drugs from a dealer in town. I couldn't believe it. Couldn't entertain the thought that she could do such a thing. I knew that drug addiction made people into something different, but how could she have turned into such a monster? Was she always a monster? If she was a monster, was there a monster inside of me too?

A few days later, I saw the arrest record. Even in her mug shot, she looked good. She had makeup on. Her skin and hair looked healthy. She wasn't smiling, but she didn't look dour.

I struggled to believe that she was a monster. Only that the drugs made her do monstrous things. Still, I knew I would feel differently if my child was one of the children she abused.

I had a PhD, stability, a good partner, and a child headed to a prestigious college. I had been through terrible things, but my life was peaceful. How had I survived such things when my childhood friend had not? There is a part of me that wonders if I was spared because I wasn't a great beauty, because I didn't attract the same kind of people my friend attracted, but this seems like a simplistic and sexist answer. The biggest difference between my friend and me is that I got out of that town, and she did not. When another friend heard the news, she said that she believes places have energy and spirits. "Our hometown has a dark energy. Hellmouth," she said.

As I looked at the mug shot in the safety of my living room in Ohio, I could see the darkness in my childhood friend's eyes. A darkness so vast and deep from which there seemed to be no exit. I'll never know whether the darkness came from my friend herself, or her family, or the town. I'll never know where my ex-husband's darkness came from either, but I saved myself from his darkness by leaving, and I saved myself from my hometown's darkness by leaving too.

That night at the guard station, when the light across the river told me I was forgiven, it wasn't lying. Sometimes the light felt out of reach, but for me, it was always there. I'm grateful for this light. For whatever is looking out for me. Tonight, I'll light a candle for my friend. I'll cast a spell into the universe that the light will find her. That the light will find her victims too.

Everything That Brings Me Joy Also Brings Me Sorrow Now

Sometimes I think my ex-husband is my shadow side—a manifestation of my own darkness. I know this is what he wants me to believe, and I do not want to give him the satisfaction, but still, there is a part of me that remains loyal to his narrative. It is the ultimate in self-betrayal. When we were married, the intimacy was such that I couldn't tell where his darkness ended, and my own began. Was it intimacy or was it complete and utter collapse? I collided against him, and I am still searching for my own remains in the rubble. Judith Herman writes in *Trauma and Recovery*, "When trust is lost, traumatized people feel that they belong more to the dead than to the living." The part of me that remains alive searches for the corpse of the woman who trusted the man who hurt her so very deeply, but she is nowhere to be found.

Emily Dickinson wrote, "One need not be a chamber—to be haunted," and I am a walking, breathing ghost. At our child drop-offs, I look over to my ex-husband's car and make eye contact with his wife. I wave. I have no idea what else to do or how else to act. She glares at me with hatred. She has to hate me to believe in her own life, but I have never been hated like this before, and I wonder if there is some kernel of truth to her hatred. If *I* am the darkness rather than *him*, then maybe *he* is different with *her*.

Stevie Smith wrote, "I was much too far out all my life / And not waving but drowning." I have been too far out for so long. I am waving. No, I am drowning. I am waving. No, I am drowning. I am waving. I am waving. I am waving. I am crying out to be saved.

The man I am sleeping with is kind and gentle. His arms are strong from rowing boats and climbing mountains, but he would never use that strength to hurt me. When he embraces me, I do not drown but float. Though I know no man can save me, when he holds me, I feel saved. It is a feeling I cannot quite comprehend.

The man I am sleeping with says to me, "You are so sweet."

"I am not sweet," I say. "You just think that because you like me."

"No," he says. "I am not the only person who thinks that you are kind. I know that you are kind. I see how you are with other people. I see how they are around you."

Something in me wants to believe him. I want to believe that I am worthy of his love, though I already know that, though he likes me, he will never love me.

Still, the part of me that remains loyal to my ex-husband's narrative remembers him calling me crazy. A *cunt*. "Don't say that word," I begged. "I don't like it." I never should have begged. My begging always gave him power.

"You fucking cunt" was his reply. Soon, that was all I knew. I knew that I was a cunt. *A cunt. A cunt. A cunt. A cunt.* I was much too far out. So far out that no one could see me waving. Only a roiling darkness where I had once been. Was it his darkness or my own? I'll never know because, by the end, it was impossible to tell.

PART 3

THE PROBLEM

Silences

That moment, just after I'd dropped my son, Reed, off at the gas station, I told him, "Bye, baby. Have a good weekend. I love you."

He replied, "I love you too," before slinging his backpack over his shoulder and walking across the Ritchie County 7-Eleven parking lot to his father's car. I cleaned my sunglasses and settled on some music. When I turned to pull out of the parking lot, I saw a man sitting on a motorcycle. He smiled at me so tenderly because he had witnessed the exchange, so I smiled back at him, then drove into the brightly setting sun and tried not to cry because tenderness is almost always my undoing.

Soon, it was just me and the silence.

Only months after the divorce, Reed was sitting in the backseat of the car, and I had yelled at him because we thought he was going to miss the school bus. I yelled something like "I cannot do this all on my own."

And, then, his silence. He was only eight. His silence said so much.

* * *

My father's silence on the phone when I told him for the first time that my ex-husband had beaten me up.

The silence of my ex-husband's friends.

The silence of my ex-husband's family.

The silence of the police officer who arrested my ex-husband just after he had asked, "Did she hit you too? Because we can arrest her too."

The silence of the Mon County victim's advocate who didn't reach out to me until the day of my ex-husband's court hearing.

The silence of a justice system that didn't tell a victim the date that her abuser was scheduled to go to court.

The silence of the prosecutor in my ex-husband's domestic battery case who dropped his charges after he agreed to write me a letter of apology.

The silence in my apartment after I read the letter and realized that *he wasn't sorry at all.*

The silence of the university that continues to employ my batterer.

My own silence for so many years.

Silence has consequences. The silence of my ex-husband's friends, his family, the victim's advocate, the prosecutor, the university, and *my own father*. All of those silences contribute to his violence.

I will no longer be silent because silence is complicity.

The silence at night, just after I left my ex-husband, when I would take half of an Ambien, then lay on a mattress on the floor of my friend's guest room and wait for darkness to overcome me.

The silence that followed the moment after my ex-husband forced an entire bottle of Ambien into my mouth, sawing open my lip with the dull edge of the pill bottle, then commanded me to swallow. I held the pills in my cheeks, but finally, I gave up. He saw it in my eyes. He knew I was ready to swallow. He punched me in the face, and the pills blew out across the bathroom floor. He said with disgust, "Look at you. Just look at you."

I thought to myself, *Look at me.*

Some things are better left silent, but I no longer know what those things are.

The silence of the students who saw my lip cut wide open, my black eye, my eyebrow split and oozing. I think I told them I tripped on the edge of a carpet.

That, too, was a silence. There was hopelessness in my self-betrayal, and the hopelessness became its own kind of silence.

My ex-husband's silence when my friend Rebecca said, "What on earth happened to your arm?"

And I fumbled, "I don't know. I think I did it in my sleep," while Caleb watched me as though he was daring me to say something.

The silence of all of the people who ignore abusers in their own circles.

The way asking victims to name themselves is its own kind of silencing. The way, in our culture, to be named as a victim is to be vulnerable because people don't like "victims." They like "survivors."

The way I did it. I named myself. I did what they asked for, but does that mean I wasn't silenced? No.

The way that people ask for names but will never support the survivors.

The way that some survivors are better off nameless because naming opens them up to further abuse, not just from their abuser, but from the enablers, the rationalizers, the apologists, and, too often, the justice system that is supposed to protect them.

The silence that doesn't acknowledge power imbalance—how hard it is to speak out against an abuser in a position of power. I was only able to speak out against my own abuser because he *has no power over me*. Not anymore, at least.

And then, different kinds of silence.

The silence of a quiet home, free of yelling, or crying, or objects being thrown.

Companionable silence.

The silence at night—in that state between wakefulness and sleep—free of Ambien, free of darkness.

The silence between my father and me that is a chosen silence: a silence that says *I forgive you*.

The silence of the wilderness in Idaho. The silence of the river trail; the silence of my footsteps; the quiet, rushing water;

the trees rustling; the crickets shivering in the grasses; the occasional rattle of a rattlesnake; the *cheep, cheep* of marmots in the rocks; all of it captured in silence.

The silence right now, as I type these words in my home and know that I am safe.

The silence of peace.

The way I responded to Reed's silence in that car by grumpily saying, "Your father yells at you all the time."

The way he said, "I know, but you don't, and that's why it hurts more when you yell at me."

The way I knew he was right, so though I was silent for a moment, it wasn't a long silence before I apologized and promised to try to be better. The way I don't ever want him to feel silenced by me, and I don't think he has. The way he trusts me and talks to me in ways I never could with my parents. The way that all of us can be better than our parents. The way that it may be too late to save myself, but maybe it's not too late to save him. The way that not knowing whether I can, or have, saved him will be a silence that haunts me until everything goes silent one final time.

Ms. Sundberg,

An internal investigation was conducted by Lieutenant [name redacted] into your allegations of inappropriate and/or unprofessional police conduct against Sergeant [name redacted] concerning UPD Incident Report #12-0016621, Domestic Battery.

Both Sergeant [name redacted] and the other involved officer, Sergeant [name redacted], were interviewed. Lt. [name redacted] also spoke with you. At the conclusion of this investigation the facts show that all applicable department policies and State of WV laws were adhered to by both of our officers. No wrongdoing was found.

At the conclusion of this investigation, I find that your complaint is unfounded.

If you need or desire additional information please schedule an appointment with Chief [name redacted] and myself at [name redacted].

Sincerely,
Major [name redacted]

Still Screaming

I was battered in a dorm at the Institution on the Hill with the Big Football Team. The man who hurt me was my husband. In the apartment where we lived and worked, on the first floor of a recently remodeled dormitory, there was a walk-in closet where I used to hide while he raged. I would climb behind the suitcases stuffed into one corner. I knew he would find me, but I would hide anyway.

I wondered how the guy who sat behind the front desk just outside of our apartment—the guy who talked too much and loved *Star Trek*—didn't hear my screams at night, despite the fact that I could hear his chair scraping back and forth across the floor.

After my husband was handcuffed—in the back parking lot to preserve his privacy—by men in black uniforms and taken away. After the EMTs examined my foot, swollen and blue. After I signed a form declining transport to the hospital. After everyone had left. After I limped to the kitchen to sweep up the ceramic shards from the bowl that only an hour earlier my husband had shattered against my body. After I collapsed onto the cold kitchen floor. After I laid my cheek on the tile and keened a low, hard cry.

And after he came home to me in that apartment and brought me crutches. And after I slept next to him that night. And after the assistant provost sat at our table the next morning and told us that the Institution had a zero-tolerance policy on violence and we would have to move out by the end of the week. And after I realized that I was a part of that "zero-tolerance" policy. And after I looked around me and knew that everything was owned by the Institution. And after I realized I had nowhere to go. And after I realized that I, too, was owned by the Institution.

After all of that, there was only more *after*. I was only ever an *after*.

Silence / Silences / Silencing / Silenced.

When I was a little girl, I had a lisp, but after years of speech therapy, I now have a sibilant *s*.

The word "silence" is sibilant; it hisses.

Survey of the Damage:
One ceramic bowl shattered.
One busted foot.
One marriage over.
One fatherless son.
One homeless mother.
One career ended (hers, not his).
One yellow flier with a list of services available to victims.

One phone call to the community domestic violence shelter.
One email from the director of residential services. She wanted her parking permit back.

I was only ever leaving. The word "leaving" implies an action, a propelling forward. I was leaving when he hit me, when he screamed at me, when he called me names. I was leaving my mind; I was leaving my body. I was leaving, but never *gone*.

I was leaving when my husband chased me into the street in front of the dormitory. I was leaving when I begged the resident assistant to call 911. I was leaving when the resident assistant laughed, then froze with his hand above the phone and said, "Wait, are you serious?" I was leaving when the resident assistant didn't call 911. I was leaving when the same resident assistant took my husband's class the following semester because everyone knew that my husband was *such a great guy*.

I was leaving when the assistant provost called me into her office. I was leaving when, although my husband had been suspended with pay from his nonteaching position, the Institution was trying to convince me to quit. I was leaving when I told the Institution, "You have no reason to fire me, and I am not quitting. I need this job to support my son. We live alone now." I was leaving when what the assistant provost seemed to perceive as strength was merely my ability to leave.

I was leaving when the assistant provost seemed to have a moment of compassion and asked me, "Is that what he did to you?" while nodding at the boot on my foot. Suddenly, I was not leaving. I was right there, and it hurt. She saw my pain, but because she didn't want to know that pain, she turned away from me. I stood up, and then I was leaving again.

Maybe it was the way the first police officer—the young one—said to me, "It's okay. People fight. Things get crazy."

Or maybe it was the Ambien.

Or maybe it was because the second police officer said to my husband, "Did she hit you? Because we can arrest her too," and I knew that he was offering my husband an out.

Or maybe it was because, every Friday afternoon, the assistant provost made me return to the apartment where my husband had battered me, and I knew that she was punishing me.

Or maybe it was the way, at one of those meetings, the resident director slammed his hand onto the counter for emphasis, and the noise startled me into a panic.

Or maybe it was the way, at every one of those meetings, I would try to *leave, leave, leave*, so that the other faculty members would not see my shaking.

Or maybe it was because, on dark nights, I would open my computer and see on the dim, blue screen that his arrest report had been scrubbed from the campus police website.

* * *

Maybe *that* made me resolve to kill myself.

Because I wanted to be *gone*: off to wherever lost things go.

Before we moved into the dormitory, my husband and I sat in the backyard of our home and watched a lunar eclipse. The moon moved slowly, but I could track it with my eyes. My husband's tender gaze beside mine.

I surrendered to the beauty.
I prayed.
I begged.
Save me.
I feared that it was a bad idea to move into the dormitory, but wasn't it a worse idea not to? Maybe I would finally be safe there.
Save me.
As I was praying, the moon moved behind the earth's shadow, and my husband reached his hand across the distance between us. His fingers grasped mine, and the darkness obliterated the light.

The moon didn't save me, and neither did the Institution. In the end, I was no longer leaving; I was the one who left.

Silence can be so loud. How to drown it out? How to quell the screams that build inside?

In her book *Truth and Repair*, Judith Herman writes, "What about those who are tasked with implementing justice but instead ally themselves with the powerful? Often, survivors will feel the bitterness of these betrayals more deeply even than the direct harms inflicted by perpetrators." My bitterness was a poison, and the only way to purge the poison was to scream.

Screams on the outside finally quelled the screams inside. I have been screaming ever since. At my ex-husband. At the Institution on the Hill with the Big Football Team. At the police officers who worked so hard to protect my ex-husband. At the assistant provost who saw me as a participant in my own victimization. I have screamed and screamed, and I will keep screaming for as long as it takes. I will scream until I have saved myself, and when I stop screaming, I will know that I screamed for all of us—the women who couldn't speak.

Winter's Burden

Living in an Appalachian hollow is like living in an embrace that is sometimes beautiful and sometimes oppressive. The landscape around me is alive and hugs my home tightly. The organic world creeps into my house. I have to lock the doors, or I wake to find them blown wide open, leaves scattered across the floor. When it rains, I hear the pattering on the skylights above me, and the sound is beautiful until I discover water pouring in through the kitchen ceiling. Reed and I have named the spiders so that we're no longer afraid of them. We have both stopped screaming when we see a bug larger than my fist. Mouse nests inhabit my drawers. The mice are particularly partial to my collection of vintage tablecloths. Once, there was a bird trapped in the wall, and as I heard its wings crashing around in a panic, I was helpless to free it.

It is sometimes hard to know whether I have an intimacy with nature or whether I am being assaulted by it.

Last winter, we were snowed in too many times. Last winter, Reed said, "I think we're going to get cabin fever again." Last winter, I was trying to write a book proposal, edit a magazine, take graduate courses, travel to conferences and speaking engagements, and meet my PhD translation requirement, all with a son who was home from school on snow days for nearly a full month. Last winter, my translation instructor told me, *Kelly, you don't get a pass,* and I cried for an entire day. Last winter, I drove through blizzards to take my son to see his father in West Virginia, but when I asked his father if his parents would watch Reed for a couple of days, he said, "I will not ask my parents to help you."

Last winter, my pipes froze. Last winter, my furnace couldn't keep up with the frigid temperatures, and Reed and I huddled next to each other under a down comforter while the temperature in the house dropped to near freezing. Last winter, my electric bill was $500 one month, my child care was just as much, and my monthly income was $1,400. Last winter, I asked Reed's father to help supplement the extra cost of child care for the snow days, and he said, "Take me to court." Last winter, I could have taken him to court and received more support, but I also knew, as well as he did, that I had neither the energy nor the time for that, so, instead, I took out student loans.

Last winter, a newish friend inexplicably ended our friendship. She said to me, "I don't like how I feel when I'm around you." Now, I no longer feel comfortable reaching out to my friends in town when I feel sad. I save my troubles for my closest friends who talk to me on the phone, but who, always, feel too, too far away.

I require a fair amount of solitude, but I also like company. Last winter, after that friend ended our friendship, our mutual friends drifted away with her, and it felt as though I had no one but myself. In *Trauma and Recovery,* Judith Herman writes,

"Over time as most people fail the survivor's exacting test of trustworthiness, she tends to withdraw from relationships. The isolation of the survivor thus persists even after she is free." Because I didn't trust my friends to be there, I stopped reaching out. Distanced myself. There is a difference between solitude and loneliness, and the loneliness was so acute. A hunger that was almost starvation. I'd still take the loneliness over my ex-husband's company. That, at least, is true.

Last winter, I told someone I cared about that I couldn't talk to him anymore. We'd met in my hometown in Idaho, and I'd fallen in love with him, but once I returned to Ohio, he lived across the country from me. It wasn't the physical distance that made me end things, though. He was never going to love me. That was just the reality.

Last winter, on the same day I told the person I cared about I couldn't talk to him anymore, my ex-husband handed me a box he had supposedly "found." It was a box full of love letters to me, from both him and former lovers. Last winter, my ex-husband fell in love with someone else. Last winter, my ex-husband must have decided he no longer needed to steal my love letters because he loved someone else. Last winter, I shoved that box of love letters into the back of a closet because I wasn't ready to part with them, but I didn't want to be reminded of them either.

Last winter, I watched the movie version of *Wild*. Although I liked the book, the movie affected me in a more visceral way. It made me want to change my life. It made me want to create something beautiful. It made me end the relationship with the man who was never going to love me back.

Last winter, I discovered that Appalachian winters can be brutal. In my experience, much of Appalachia is brutal. I am conflating Appalachia and my ex-husband; I know this is unfair.

Tonight, I took the trash outside and stopped. The air was crisp and cold. I could smell the smoke from my neighbor's wood stove. The stars hung above me, so silver. I shivered in that cold and remembered my winters in Idaho. Winter was my favorite season then. The smell of the wood smoke. The sound of the snow. The way, when we skied, the snow muffled every sound except the *whoosh, whoosh* of our skis. The way the sound of a clump of snow falling to the ground from a tree branch was so familiar. The crunch of snowshoes up a mountainside. Snow so dry that, with the proper clothing, I could comfortably sit in it, even sleep in it. The feeling of sitting in hot springs right next to icicles. The sound of my father stoking the wood stove in the hours before dawn broke. The way our house was always warm. The gurgle of the coffee machine. The door opening to let the dog out. The muffled sound of the morning news. The feeling of having a father in my home. Oh God, how did I not know that I was lucky just to have a father in my home? That my own child wouldn't even have that?

I fell in love with my ex-husband during an Idaho winter. He lived in the country with a married couple, and the husband was an alcoholic who slept with any woman who would sleep with him, while his wife was a beautiful, gentle, doomed soul. When my ex-husband and I had breakfast with that married couple, the wife looked at me with such pity that I realized she thought that *I* was the doomed one. The truth is that we were both right. We were both doomed. If I can give any woman a single piece of relationship advice, it's this: If a woman looks at you with pity or seems sad for you, then run from the person you are with, because we know. *We know.*

I've been trying to forgive my ex-husband, but I can't. These Appalachian winters have been too hard, have made me so angry, and the truth is that anger has been my protection. The problem with coparenting with my abuser is that I can't cut out contact. I can't pretend he doesn't exist. There is no silver lining in raising a child with my abuser, so I keep my anger close. I don't know if it holds me hostage or I hold it hostage.

The anger has to go somewhere, so I put on my running shoes and a hoody, then run down the deserted road of the hollow. The air is so cold that I see my breath in front of me. The cold gets into my lungs, expands in my veins like icicles. My legs pump harder. If I run fast enough, maybe I can outrun the pain. Anger propels me forward. The anger is both my burden and my power. I am not ready to let it go, so I carry it with me into the darkness.

The Problem

I grew up always trying to be nice, to please. I carried this into my twenties. One boss, a redhead herself, said to me, "Kelly, you are the only redhead I've ever met who doesn't have a temper." She and I are friends now, and she would not say the same. In the years that have passed, I have gone from being agreeable to being a complainer.

In her book *Complaint*, Sara Ahmed writes, "To be heard as complaining is not to be heard. To hear someone as complaining is an effective way of dismissing someone . . . To be heard as making a tiresome complaint is to be heard as being tiresome, as distracting somebody from doing '*important work elsewhere*.'"

Ahmed then writes, "You can become a complainer because of where you locate the problem. To become a complainer is to become the location of the problem."

I am the problem.

It wasn't being abused that made me the problem. It wasn't leaving my abusive marriage that made me the problem. It was the act of *speaking* that made me the problem.

When I had just defended my dissertation, my advisor took me out for a drink. He had never done that before with me—likely because faculty drinking with students was frowned upon.

Faculty drinking with students was frowned upon because of a faculty member who had plied his students with alcohol, then sexually assaulted two of them. They filed a complaint, and the report that came back found that, not only had he sexually assaulted those two women, he had a long-standing pattern of such behavior. How did the department deal with the problem they had at hand? They held a vote to strip the assailant of tenure, and a good number of the faculty—almost half of them, including many women—voted for him to keep his tenure.

The people who voted for him to keep his tenure voted that way because to their minds, *the assailant* wasn't the problem. His drinking was the problem. Drinking with students was the problem. *The students themselves* were the problem. I wasn't there on the night that those women were sexually assaulted. I barely even knew them, but I was used to being the problem, so I complained, both for and with them—loudly and regularly—and sure enough, I became a problem too. There is very little that makes someone feel more alone than being in a community where they are the problem. Becoming the problem broke my heart.

How else did the department deal with the problem they had at hand? By requiring the graduate students to attend a mandatory Title IX training meeting. Faculty, absolving themselves of being the problem, were not required to attend their own. The meeting was to discuss sexual misconduct, and the rights and responsibilities we had as graduate students. I'll admit that, when I walked in and saw who was leading it, I was disappointed. I wasn't the only one. My friend whispered sarcastically, "It's nice to see a man here to talk to us about sexual harassment." I, too, felt uncomfortable that it was a man, but I didn't want to jump to conclusions.

He had a buzz cut. He was wearing khakis. He said to us, "Do you want to be here?" (I did want to be there.) Someone answered "no," but it wasn't because we didn't want the discussion. It was because we didn't want the situation that had prompted it. He said, "Well, maybe that goes both ways." I was stunned. Had he really just said that? It was oddly antagonistic. Then, he said, "That was a joke."

It was a bad joke.

He then started to tell us about the history of Title IX, and his enthusiasm was on par with how I feel about large spiders and mayonnaise, meaning nonexistent. He said, "We drew straws, and I got the short one, so I ended up with this job." Again, I was stunned. The other graduate students shifted in their seats. Made eye contact with each other, then looked down at their desks. No one said anything though.

Whether it was from watching female faculty members who claimed to be feminists remain allied with a man who did the *exact same thing* to two of our graduate students that Donald Trump bragged about in his famous "locker room talk," or whether it was from hearing the tales of senior male faculty members berating women graduate students in their offices, or whether it was the many hours of productivity lost to secret meetings and letters, all of the graduate students suffered, and yet, we were being treated as though we were the problem.

In her book *Sex Crimes: Ten Years on the Front Lines Prosecuting Rapists and Confronting Their Collaborators,* author Alice Vachss applied the term "collaborator" to describe someone who enables a predator to continue damaging others. Collaboration can happen in a variety of ways. It can be active or passive. Defending the predator is collaboration. Not filing a valid complaint against the predator is collaboration. Rationalizing the predator's behavior is collaboration. Minimizing the predator's behavior is collaboration. Delegitimizing the victims is collaboration.

A male faculty member who I was very fond of said to me, "We just feel like the graduate students made up their mind about his guilt before all of the evidence came out."

How could I respond to that?

I stared at him for a while, then finally said, "We did." We'd made up our minds because we believed our peers; that didn't seem irrational to me.

In the end, the assailant was forced to resign, and then, he and the university were sued by the women he assaulted. There was a settlement, and I was glad that the women received some kind of justice, but I also knew their lives were irrevocably changed. And witnessing so many people I admired immediately leap to disbelieve the victims damaged my faith in my department, in the institution of academia, and in humanity.

When things calmed down, my advisor, who never treated me as a problem and always treated me with respect, took me out for a drink because I passed my dissertation defense and was technically no longer his student. I expressed fear that I wouldn't get an academic job, that I had a reputation for being difficult. He looked at me straight on and said, "You are one of the easiest grad students I have ever worked with. You are not difficult." I sat with that, a bit surprised. By then, so many people had said I was difficult that I believed it.

In the last decade, I have leaned into being difficult, into being the problem. I have leaned into boundaries, and sometimes my boundaries have become an electric fence, which made *them* the problem, so I have also leaned into learning how to be a problem while staying tender because the two are not in opposition. I can be both.

Like most people, but particularly survivors, I want to be liked. Want approval. Still, I want authenticity more, so I've resigned myself to being the problem, and in the midst of being the problem, I've discovered the relationships that remain are the most pure and steadfast.

I regularly lament my reputation to my best friend who, unlike me, is universally well-liked. She has not lived what I've lived, has not felt my experience, but she believes me and believes *in* me. She regularly reminds me that I'm lovable, that I'm believable, that I am not the problem.

The biggest gift that you can give a survivor is to believe them.

Another friend, who is one of the kindest, most community-minded writers I know, regularly tells me how much she values my loyalty, my fierceness, the way I hold those I love close. She, too, is a survivor. We are bound together by the harshness of our experiences and the deep love we have found within that wake.

Yesterday, a woman said to me, "You are changing lives."

To be the problem is to change lives.

To be a mirror is also to change lives.

The people who see you as you really are? They listen with what Ahmed calls the "feminist ear." They mirror to you that the real problem is the abuse, or the assault, or the discrimination, or the racism, or the everyday kind of diminishment that eats away at your soul.

The people who have been my mirrors have changed my life.

Complain about the problem, and the world will make you the problem. There is grief in realizing that you can never go back, that you will never again not be the problem, but there is liberation contained within the same realization. Too many of us will be given the chance to be the problem. All of us will be given the chance to be a mirror. When you are given that chance, I hope you take it. Be both the problem and a mirror.

When You Blame Amber Heard, You Blame Me Too

I am haunted by the photograph of Amber Heard sobbing in her car after leaving the courtroom where she was granted a restraining order against Johnny Depp. I see her hand in front of her open mouth, eyes squeezed shut, cheeks shiny. She appears to be gasping. The vision of Heard's face has stayed with me. The photo hurts. I have cried those same tears.

Even after the divisive trial, I believe Heard. Her story is too familiar for me not to. I was not married to a celebrity, nor was I a supermodel. My abuser and I were decidedly average. Still, like Depp, my abuser was beloved by nearly everyone who knew him. My abuser was regarded as kind and gentle, always willing to help those in need, a man who listened more than he talked, who offered hugs freely, and who knew how to make everyone around him feel special.

None of those characteristics kept him from hitting me, but they did keep other people from believing me.

In many ways, my abuser was more likable than I was, so when he was arrested for domestic battery, it was a shock to those who knew us both. I had carefully protected him—not out of some kind of ulterior motive, but out of love. Hope was a drug that kept me tethered to the man who hurt me. Hope was a drug that was hard to kick.

This is why it is so difficult for me to observe the way the media and the American public talked about Heard during and after her American defamation trial with her abuser in 2022. Many of the things that have been said about her were also said about me. I am part of a community of survivors, and we are hurting. The things we are hearing—that she is manipulative and opportunistic, that she didn't get along with his family, that *she* was the abusive one—hurt us because *we have already heard it*. We heard the same stuff when we left our own abusers. The narrative is the common ground that all survivors stand on.

I don't know Amber Heard, nor do I know whether or not she is a good person, but it does not matter if she is a good person. She was abused, and that, to me, is clear. The video of Johnny Depp ranting and banging around the kitchen is enough evidence for me because breaking and throwing things is physical intimidation, and physical intimidation *is* domestic violence. The term "mutual abuse" was bandied about a lot during and after the trial, but mutual abuse does not exist. Abuse is fundamentally about control. Even if both people behave badly, in an abusive relationship, one person always has more control than the other.

Bad people can be abused, and it is still abuse. Abuse is always, in any context, wrong. I am not saying that Amber Heard is a bad person; I don't believe that. I think she behaved like someone who was being abused, and there is very little that is worse than being a survivor who is angry about their abuse while knowing that there are folks who see that anger as the *reason* they were abused. When I wrote about the trial on Twitter, I received vile messages from strangers. They seemed not to know that, in their attempts to defend an abuser, they were abusing *me*.

When I started speaking out about domestic violence, some of the most hateful people to me were other survivors. I have a theory that some people who never got to speak out about their own traumas struggle with believing people who do. Patriarchy already pits women against each other—makes us think that resources are limited—and if one woman gets to speak out and be believed, then how might that feel to another who is still suffering in silence? The reality is that not everyone has the same kind of freedom to speak out after abuse. I can imagine that, if I was silent because I knew I'd be disbelieved, it might be easier for me to disbelieve someone who was actively speaking out.

After I left my abuser, a woman wrote to me, "You're hurting the cause with your anger." I still hear those words: "You're hurting the cause with your anger. You're hurting the cause with your anger." Years later, I suddenly realized that she and I never shared a cause.

Time passes, wounds heal, and people move on, but some things never stop hurting. For me, and so many other survivors, being blamed for our abuse will never stop hurting.

I could list the other ways my story resembles Heard's. That, although my abuser was arrested, I did not want to press charges. That I was more interested in protecting him and our privacy than I was in protecting myself. That the police did not look for injuries when they first arrived at my home. That the police failed to recognize the extent of my suffering. That, although the police did eventually discover my injuries and had to arrest him, I never felt that they had any protective motivations. That there were far more incidents in the history of my marriage where the injuries were not visible. That bruises, so often, do not materialize until the next day. That the moment I left my abuser was not triumphant; rather, it was a moment of face-contorting tears. That I, too, smiled in the days after I left, but not because I was happy. I smiled because, by then, I knew how to smile through suffering.

There are even more similarities, but I am no longer interested in asserting my legitimacy as a victim. Instead, I am interested in asserting my value as a woman who deserves to be believed, in asserting the value of all of us—the more than a third of all women in the United States—who have experienced domestic violence.

I have been thinking a lot about values. I value kindness, but kindness only goes so far. What I value more is integrity, and integrity does not begin until those who are kind actually stand behind their values. While Heard was being retraumatized in court, and so many women were experiencing that with her, I was getting acupuncture for my stress. One day, I told the acupuncturist that I was stressed because of the trial. "The question is then," he said, "why are you following it?"

I thought about it, then said, "Because I believe her, and I want to honor her."

There is a scene in the movie *Room* where, after a woman and her young son break free from years of captivity, the boy's grandfather keeps his head turned away from the grandson he has only recently met. The grandfather cannot bear to look; he squeezes his eyes shut, so he does not have to be a witness to this living reminder of his daughter's suffering and what it bore. The grandfather's refusal to look is an act of cowardice. In order to bear witness, we must *look*. Bearing witness means acknowledging what has happened, that it is unequivocally wrong, and that it was not the victim's fault. Bearing witness hurts, but is necessary. It is necessary for Heard, it is necessary for me, and it is necessary for the millions of other survivors of domestic violence in our country. We need you to open your eyes. We need you to look at us. I tell myself that, when you see us, things will change. I tell myself that, when you see us, you'll finally believe us.

Where Were the Mothers like Me?

After my son's birth, I was wheeled out of the hospital with tears streaming down my face. I'm still not sure why I was crying, because I felt nothing. My mother looked at me and said kindly, "Someone has the baby blues."

I thought, *I'm not blue. I'm nothing.* I thought, *The world is gray now.*

That's how the world felt for a long time: affectless, flat. I, too, was affectless, and flat. I don't have fondness anymore for my ex-husband, but I do feel compassion for what he must have experienced with a newborn son and a wife whose body suddenly seemed like an empty container with no soul left inside of it.

I was never officially diagnosed with postpartum depression, but a year later, I started antidepressants. They didn't help. The world only became grayer, more muted, more two-dimensional. Looking back, it's difficult to know whether I had postpartum depression or was depressed because I had married a man who would alter the course of my life with his fists. I understand a little bit more about intuition now, and I understand why I sobbed the night before my wedding, just as I later cried in that wheelchair. Though my rational brain didn't want to see it yet, my intuitive brain knew I was walking my own gauntlet when I married the man who would later abuse me.

When I got pregnant, I wasn't ready to have a child. I didn't even know if I *wanted* children. I was terrified of having a relationship with my child like my mother had with me. Our relationship was fraught, and at that point in my life, it was my biggest source of pain. It was hard for me to dream of a mother-child relationship that looked different.

In an MFA workshop, a visiting fiction writer once said, "A pox on tears!" It was lazy, she said, to describe a woman's emotional state via tears. We could, she said, be more creative than that.

This is my disclaimer: A pox on tears!

And this is where I say that, when the pregnancy test revealed two lines, I broke into tears. Tears are always a warning for me. They know what I can't yet see. They know what I feel intuitively. They knew I wasn't ready to be a mother.

Despite the flatness of the early days of his life, I always loved my son. He was perfect. His face round and symmetrical. His eyes big and bright. His personality, even as a baby, larger than it should have been. And now, many years later, he has turned into an exceptional teenager who is beloved by everyone who knows him, who has a 4.0 GPA at a magnet school for gifted and talented kids, who is funny, who respects me, and who I love more than anyone else in the world. Every day, I feel relief that, together, he and I have come so far. I feel relief that he's different from me, and that I'm different from my mother.

Always, in my heart, there is this sense that I was *lucky*. That whatever higher power exists, that higher power recognized that I needed a child like him, that I was spared a child like the kind of child I was.

I was an unruly child. Not bad hearted, but a poor listener who lacked discipline. A daydreamer. Chaotic. Wild. The more my mother tried to control me, the more I failed at being the kind of kid she wanted, and the worse I felt about myself.

I was forty-four when I was finally diagnosed with ADHD, and as I drove home from the doctor's office, I called my mother and cried. I think she cried too. I'm sure that we both wondered how things could have been different if we'd known.

A pox on tears!

My son's delivery was traumatic, and I was unconscious at one point. A friend had recommended that I take advantage of the hospital and use that time to catch up on rest, so I asked the nurses to keep my son in the nursery while I slept and bring him to me for breastfeeding when he was hungry. I slept feverishly. Painfully. At one point, I woke to voices in the hallway outside my door.

A nurse said, "Why is that baby in the nursery?"
Another nurse said, "Her labor was really hard."
"But he's her *baby*," the first nurse said.

That was the first time I felt the shame of being a mother. The shame of knowing that, from that point forward, any time I put myself first, I would be failing my child.

It will never be enough, I told myself. *I will ruin his life.* My only parenting philosophy has been this: *Do your very best not to ruin his life.*

A few years ago, I had a spat with a very famous woman writer. I had shared an essay by Michael Chabon on social media about all of the books he had written despite his many children. I said something to the effect of "This is not the voice we need in the world when it comes to parenting and the writing life."

My comment was not a criticism of Michael Chabon as an individual or writer. He's an exceptionally good writer who obviously has a very good heart. I suspect he is also a very good parent, but as a single mom living off of a $15,000-a-year stipend while in graduate school, I did not think his story of parenting—one I perceived as privileged (he surely had nannies)—was necessary. "Where were the parenting writers like me?" I asked in my post. "The single moms? The working-class parents?"

Another writer commented that those writers didn't have time to write think pieces about parenting and the writing life, and I vowed to write one myself, but then the very famous writer who had no children came into my comments. She was good friends with Michael Chabon. She told me, among other angry things, that she was tired of watching me "decide who was privileged and who was not." Maybe she was right, but she was a famous writer, and I was only a grad student. I deleted the post, and I never wrote that essay about parenting and the writing life. My inner voice said, *People aren't interested in stories by mothers like me.*

The town where I completed my PhD was small and parochial. There weren't many mothers like me, and it was lonely. Single mothers were treated with distrust, and when my son played soccer in the third grade, the other mothers mostly didn't speak to me. The fathers would speak to me when their wives weren't around, which sounds like a cliché, but my experience was that married mothers can be wary of single mothers. Maybe they have good reasons for that.

My son wasn't very good at soccer; he didn't have a dad to kick the ball around with, and I certainly didn't know how to be that for him. Like me, he didn't have many friends, which was hard to watch. A divorced father took pity on me and made conversation with me (divorced fathers weren't treated like the divorced mothers were). We stood on the sidelines, and I lost track of the game, when I heard him say, "Is that your son?" I looked, and my son was on the ground. As my little boy stood up, all of the kids took a knee. He stood in the middle of those children kneeling around him, his little face so confused.

I asked the father what happened. "I think the ball hit him in the face," he said. "They take a knee when a kid is injured." I looked at my boy. He was so confused, but also clearly honored by the attention, and I fought not to cry. I fought not to feel like I had failed him completely because I hadn't given him a father who would teach him how to catch a ball. Despite my efforts, I cried, just a little. The father looked at me kindly. "He's okay," he said.

A pox on tears!

After I finished my PhD, I went on the academic job market, and there were four jobs in my field that year. A Midwestern Christian school brought me to campus, and I could tell they were excited about me, but I didn't feel it was a fit. I cried in the car on my drive home (my intuition knew). I asked my dissertation advisor what to do if they offered me the job, and he said, "Kelly, you have a child to support. You can't be turning jobs down." He was right. After I accepted the position, he said to me, "Don't be yourself." He was kidding but only a little, and he was right. I have spent almost five years now being someone else because who I am, a queer feminist, isn't compatible with the beliefs of the institution.

Do you know how hard it is to try and be someone else for five years?

I accepted the job, but I chose not to live in the conservative small town where the school is. Instead, I moved to a nearby city, and I commute to my small college. My son has found his place in an urban magnet school full of queer and neurodivergent kids. He is happy and thriving and completely *himself*. I would do it all again for his happiness. *Don't ruin his life*, my conscience chides me, so I choose not to apply for jobs out of the area, not to move him again. I choose to put his needs first because that is the responsibility I took on when I made the decision to have him.

✢ ✢ ✢

This semester, the president of my institution said that he was planning on actively discriminating against LGBTQ folks because they do not fit with the mission of the school, and after five years of exploitation, I finally decided to step away from my position. This is a luxury that has been afforded me because my son received a full-ride scholarship to a good college nearby, and my now live-in partner has offered to support me for a while. If I was still a single mother, I could not have made this choice.

Always, single mothers have to make decisions, but we don't often get "choices." There is a difference.

Someone who was close to me during my PhD program, and who now has her own child, said to me recently, "I don't know how you did it."

I thought, *I don't know how I did it either.* Then I started crying.

A pox on tears!

As hard as single parenting has been, I have written two books in that time. Still, I want to ask Michael Chabon how many books I could have written in those ten years if I wasn't raising a child alone.

In her beautiful meditation on class and the writing life titled *Silences*, Tillie Olsen writes, "More than in any human relationship, overwhelmingly more, motherhood means being instantly interruptible. It is distraction, not meditation, that becomes habitual; interruption, not continuity." I wrote at night after my son went to sleep. I wrote in the afternoons when he was in the after-school program that I couldn't afford. I wrote when he was at his father's house every other weekend. I wrote when he was sick next to me on the couch. I didn't date, didn't have a social life, didn't spend much time with anyone but my son. I wrote and wrote and wrote, but always, I was instantly interruptible, and when I looked at the other parents around me, I thought, *Where are the mothers like me?*

For a while, I had a friend who was also a single mom. We were fast and close for a couple of years, but we grew apart. Her parents lived nearby and would stay with her son for weeks at a time so that she could visit her long-distance boyfriend. She received more from spousal and child support than my entire monthly salary and child support combined. She was able to go out to bars and restaurants and parties. She was very talented, but also active on social media, and she regularly portrayed her success as a matter of hard work and grit. Though she was certainly hard-working, there is no way around the reality that she also had a lot of unacknowledged privilege. *I know, I know. Who am I to decide who has privilege?!* I knew she was inspiring to other single parents, but I grew to resent her, and my resentment embarrassed me. I didn't want to be that kind of person.

A friend recently told me that her therapist says resentment is always rooted in envy, and I realize that's true. I resented Michael Chabon's piece because I envied his financial circumstances and his co-parent and his probable nannies. I resented my then friend because I envied her spousal and child support, as well as her attentive parents who lived nearby. Maybe I envied her talent too, because I'm sure I'm not the only one who read her social media posts about her productivity and wondered what was wrong with me that I was not able to produce at that speed.

And though I cannot and should not be the privilege police, I do know this: She happily turned down many paychecks in favor of her writing time, which I both envied and resented because until I chose to resign from my academic position, I had never knowingly stepped away from a paycheck in my life.

A few summers ago, my son went to a free creative writing camp hosted by a local university. One of his instructors at the creative writing camp, an MFA student, was surprised when she learned that I'm his mom.

"Mom," he said. "She knew who you were when I said your book title! She didn't even need me to say your name." He was clearly surprised and thrilled and also seemed to think it was a little funny.

"Are you famous?" his friend asked.

"No," I said, explaining that the literary world is small, and that we tend to know each other.

But I was proud. I was proud that my son was able to see that all the sacrifices we'd made together weren't for nothing, that his patience with me as I wrote for all of those years created this world that makes his world better too.

The creative writing camp students all did a reading at the capstone event, and my son was so confident, so clear, and so, so funny. *How is that my kid?* I wondered. *Where did this confidence come from?*

Maybe I'm just a better parent for a teenager than a baby. Maybe I'm just no longer in an abusive marriage. Maybe I'm no longer poor (though still lower middle-class), but the world is no longer gray. It's no longer flat. It's no longer two-dimensional. I am writing the work I want to see into the world. My beautiful son is thriving. Though I floundered and failed in so many ways, somehow, I haven't yet ruined his life and I know that none of that time with my son, the love of my life, was wasted. I asked so many times, "Where were the mothers like me?" Still, the answer never mattered. I can't be Michael Chabon. I can't be my former friend. I can't be the very famous woman writer. I can only be who I am, and I am the mother like me.

Everything That Brings Me Joy Also Brings Me Sorrow Now

I am in bed with my lover surrounded by white. Clean white sheets, pillows, duvet. We are in a hotel that is more than we can afford on our own, but we aren't paying for it because I gave the keynote address for a domestic violence organization in Coeur d'Alene, Idaho. I opened the address by saying, "The last time I was in Coeur d'Alene was on my honeymoon with the man who would later batter me." This felt like a triumphant moment, *was* a triumphant moment, but after the speech, after the applause, after the hugs from other tearful survivors, after my lover and I rode on a boat back to our hotel, after the sunlight was so beautiful I almost cried, after a woman on the boat said, "Did you just get married?," after we laughed as we said no, after we took the same boat to a private infinity pool at this resort we *could not afford on our own*, after we stood in the pool and watched the blue of the pool meet the blue of the lake meet the blue of the horizon, after I thought of how Rebecca Solnit once wrote that the blue of distance is the blue of desire, after I suddenly understood what those words meant, after I floated in that blue for as long as I could, after we returned to our room where we fucked on those clean white sheets, after I looked at my lover resting his head tenderly on my chest. After all of that, I call my lover the name of my abuser because in that moment, all bound up in blue and white, time is so permeable. I slip back and forth between the past and the present, and it is all the same. The lover of my past is the lover of my present, but no, of course they aren't the same, but they feel the same. I am the same. Isn't that what matters? That I am the same? That I may have escaped my abuser, but I can never escape myself? Judith Herman writes in *Trauma and Recovery*, "The reconstruction of trauma requires immersion in a past experience of frozen time; the descent into mourning feels like a surrender to tears that are endless." But I have already descended into mourning, have cried endless tears, have moved beyond the frozen time and into a present that, despite all of my emotional work, is vast and unknowable and terrifying.

My psychic therapist later says she understands how I could confuse my lover and abuser, that she understands why I would slip back and forth in time in that moment. So much of magic is basic psychology that treats the experience as real rather than in our heads. My real therapist would say it's natural for me to *feel* as though I am slipping back and forth in time. The psychic therapist says it's natural that I *am* slipping back and forth in time. Such a subtle difference, and yet, an infinite division. My lover, a scientist, says psychology is a soft science anyway; he never dismisses my interest in magic. The psychic therapist reminds me that my lover is not like my abuser, and I believe her because she is psychic, because I need to believe something, because I can't believe myself, because I am not to be trusted, because I am the one who married the abuser, because I am the one who let him hurt me, because I am the same, I am the same, I am the same. New day, new man, same me.

Later, I tell the psychic therapist that my abuser appeared to me in a dream. He said, "I see now how wrong I was." I tell her that it felt real, that I felt peace when I woke up. "Your karmic ties to each other are resolved," she says. "You can let go now." And I do. In some subtle way, I let go, but if I let go, then what do I have left? Herman writes about the process of letting go: "Her grief, too, begins to lose its vividness. It occurs to the survivor that perhaps the trauma is not the most important, or even the most interesting, part of her life story. At first these thoughts may seem almost heretical. The survivor may wonder how she can possibly give due respect to the horror she has endured if she no longer devotes her life to remembrance and mourning." I know I am a traitor to my own horror, that all of the love I let into my life in the present betrays my grief, asks it to fade into the past, but the past is the present, and the present is the past, and the future is nothing, so I ask my grief if I can just get a little break? I tell my grief that I will continue to honor it, but I want to feel love in the meantime. I tell my grief that I want to be happy. *Please, grief*, I ask, *I promise to always honor this sorrow, but let me feel joy in the meantime. Let me believe in this magic.*

PART 4

LOVE & RAGE

The Witching Hour

Red is blood. Red is cherries—sweet, firm. Red is chiles, red is heat. I once stood in rural Belgium at the edge of a field full of strawberries, and while the wind blew through the green leaves of the red berry plants, the clouds cleaved above me, and I felt a cleaving too—a grief that let go, but only for a moment.

The garnet is my home state's gemstone. I have a star garnet sitting next to me now because it is supposed to enhance creativity and strength. I hold the stone in my palm, stroke it with my thumb and find that it is both smooth and warm.

Red is the witch—burned at the stake. Red is the succubus—killing men with their own desires.

My friend's father used to call me "Red" because of my hair. He wore red flannel shirts, cut down trees for a living, and killed animals for sport. My cheeks flushed red when he called me that.

Red is an alarm. Red is a stop sign, stoplight, and most other forms of *stop*.

I married a man who loves redheads. His hair, too, was red. His nose red from alcohol. His fists red from hitting me. His cheeks red from shame.

I was the witch, the succubus. I was also the stop sign, the stoplight. I said, *Stop*. I said, *Please stop*. I said, *Oh God, please make him stop*.

The witching hour arrives at night. Night is when I sit on the couch in the dark, and while my son sleeps quietly in his bedroom, the ghosts get in. Their voices taunt me.

I say, *Oh God, please make them stop*.

Ghosts:

My ex-husband, Caleb's, voice says, "I would not be this way with another woman. It must be you who brings this out in me."

His friend's voice says, "I heard that you *beat up on each other*."

His mother's voice says, "Just put your troubles at the foot of the cross."

My father's voice says, "Kelly, I just don't know what to believe."

I say, *I expected better from you. And you. And you*. I say, *Father, I needed better from you*. No one hears me because I am too angry. My anger is proving them all right.

My therapist says, "I'd be worried about you if you *weren't* angry." My best friend says, "I knew you before. I know this anger is not who you are." My mother says, "You are so funny. Why can't you write something lighthearted for a change? You have all of those funny stories." I don't know how to tell my mother that those stories came from before, and, now, I will only ever be an *after*.

* * *

I repeat the adage to myself: "Anger is like taking poison, then waiting for the other person to die." I am still waiting for him to die.

When I was a little girl, I was often told I had a "redheaded temper." A boy on the bus called me "Carrot Top." He pulled my ponytail—made fun of my body, my shyness, my awkwardness. I was in the third grade, already learning that feeling of hating myself, that pervading sadness. This was before my mom would say it was as if I went into my bedroom and never came back out. Once I learned what sadness felt like, I never knew how to feel any differently.

That boy on the bus pushed me. Knocked the wind out of me. I had already learned not to push boys back; I already knew what force would come back at me if I did. So I did something else. I got a pitcher from my house, opened the fridge, and I poured as many disgusting things in that pitcher as I could find: orange juice, Worcestershire sauce, mustard, stale Riesling from a forgotten wine bottle in the back. I let the pitcher ferment in my closet for a week, and then, one morning, I hid the pitcher in my backpack and carried my pack in my arms so that it didn't spill. I left my pack, pitcher inside, on the floor of my classroom all day underneath the hook that had my name on it. When I got off the bus that afternoon, the boy turned to taunt me, but instead of running away from him, I walked toward him. I reached into my backpack, and he must have seen something in my eyes.

He turned and ran but couldn't stop looking back at me. I pulled the pitcher out and tossed the liquid in his direction. It missed him entirely and splashed back up on my own arm instead. He pointed at me and laughed but kept running. From then on, whenever he saw me, he'd shout, "She's crazy. You'd better run!"

But he never picked on me again.

And I got it, I understood. A girl has two options: She can be a victim, or she can be crazy.

After my divorce, when I decided not to be a victim anymore, the only other option was to be seen as crazy.

Caleb's crazy ex-wife. Caleb's crazy ex-wife. Caleb's crazy ex-wife. Caleb's crazy ex-wife. Caleb's crazy ex-wife. Caleb's crazy ex-wife. Caleb's crazy ex-wife. Caleb's crazy ex-wife. Caleb's crazy ex-wife. Caleb's crazy ex-wife.

His friend, the rape survivor's, voice says, "What were *your* *triggers* that led you to stay with him when it got so bad?" My friend, the feminist's, voice says, "You are hurting 'the cause' with your anger." Our friend's voice says, "I can still be friends with both of you. I don't need to take sides." I say, *What about his triggers that led him to be violent?* I say, *What are you doing for the cause with your silence?* I say, *If you care about me, then how can you be friends with the man who hurt me?* But I don't ask these questions out loud. They float into the night.

The assistant prosecutor dismissed the domestic battery charges against my ex-husband, Caleb, rather than go to trial on January 24, 2014. I was in the first year of my PhD program.

My eight-year-old son had a snow day from school, so I bundled him up, held his mitten-clad hand in mine, and together, we picked our way across the snowy campus to a mandatory meeting for all of the PhD students. I had no idea Caleb was in court. No one had even told me there was a hearing scheduled. I received a phone call on my way into the meeting. The victim's advocate wanted to know if the assistant prosecutor could dismiss the charges rather than go to trial. I had not been given any time to prepare, had no idea what to say, so I said yes. It wasn't what I wanted.

I went into the meeting and sat surrounded by graduate students who knew nothing about the call I had just fielded so naively, who knew nothing about what or where or how I was. My son kicked his legs in the desk next to me, leaned back in his seat, and looked up at the ceiling. My gaze followed his. I stared at a ceiling tile, stained from moisture, and tried not to cry. My eyes watered anyway; the stain on the ceiling darkened in my vision until I saw only red.

Later, when I fought to get the assistant prosecutor to go back and do her job right, she brought up the day Caleb had been arrested. I had slept without underwear. I was still without it when I woke in the morning and went to the kitchen to confront him about his abuse. I told him I was leaving him. I turned to walk away, and he yelled, "Don't turn your butt to me!" I leaned over and gave a little butt wave at him. He threw a ceramic bowl at me that busted my foot and resulted in his arrest.

✶   ✶   ✶

The assistant prosecutor's voice says, "How was I supposed to convince a jury he was guilty when you shook your bare butt at him?"

I say, "Are you saying this is my fault? Was I not allowed to be angry at my abusive husband?"

But there is another voice in this particular story. I had complained to the assistant prosecutor's boss, the district prosecutor, about the mishandling of my case. We are on a conference call about this, and the district prosecutor jumps in. "No one is saying that," she says. "We would never say that."

Still, the ghost of the assistant prosecutor has already found a home in my own voice: *It was my fault. It was my fault. It was my fault. It was my fault.*

He would not have been like this with another woman. He would not have been like this with another woman. He would not have been like this with another woman. He would not have been like this with another woman.

The district prosecutor's voice says, "On behalf of the state of West Virginia, I'd like to offer you an apology. I hope this gives you closure."

I say, "Thank you." I am crying. There is no closure.

Later, when I'm driving my son to spend the weekend with his dad, and I cross the bridge over the wide, muddy Ohio River, the sign reads, WELCOME TO WEST VIRGINIA! WILD AND WONDERFUL! and I say, *West Virginia, you should be sorry.*

When I see Caleb in his car, and he can't look at me, I say, *Caleb, you should be sorry.*

When Caleb brings his new girlfriend on one of those drives, and I wave at her out of politeness, but she glares at me as though I am a witch, I say, *Someday, he will make you sorry.* And I feel sorry for her too, but not so sorry that I'm not angry. In fact, I'm so angry that I'm shaking as I drive home, but then, as I near that bridge across the Ohio River, the clouds cleave again. The sky behind them is not blue. It is red. Stoplight red. Heart monitor red. My heart hurts. I sob alone into the silence of my car.

To see red is to be overwhelmed by anger, out of control. Blinded.

Red Red Red Red Red Red Red Red Red Red Red Red Red
Red Red Red Red Red Red Red Red Red Red Red Red Red
Red Red Red Red Red Red Red Red Red Red Red Red Red
Red Red Red Red Red Red Red Red Red Red Red Red Red
Red Red Red Red Red Red Red Red Red Red Red Red Red
Red Red Red Red Red Red Red Red Red Red Red Red Red
Red Red Red Red Red Red Red Red Red Red Red Red Red
Red Red Red Red Red Red Red Red Red Red Red Red Red
Red Red Red Red Red Red Red Red Red Red Red Red Red
Red Red Red Red Red Red Red Red Red Red Red Red Red
Red Red Red Red Red Red Red Red Red Red Red Red Red
Red Red Red Red Red Red Red Red Red Red Red Red Red
Red Red Red Red Red Red Red Red Red Red Red Red Red
Red Red Red Red Red Red Red Red Red Red Red Red Red
Red Red Red Red Red Red Red Red Red Red Red Red Red
Red Red Red Red Red Red Red Red Red Red Red Red Red

Red Red Red Red Red Red Red Red Red Red Red Red Red
Red Red Red Red Red Red Red Red Red Red Red Red Red
Red Red Red Red Red Red Red Red Red Red Red Red Red
Red Red Red Red Red Red Red Red Red Red Red Red Red
Red Red Red Red Red Red Red Red Red Red Red Red Red
Red Red Red Red Red Red Red Red Red Red Red Red Red
Red Red Red Red Red Red Red Red Red Red Red Red Red
Red Red Red Red Red Red Red Red Red Red Red Red Red
Red Red Red Red Red Red Red Red Red Red Red Red Red
Red Red Red Red Red Red Red Red Red Red Red Red Red
Red Red Red Red Red Red Red Red Red Red Red Red Red
Red Red Red Red Red Red Red Red Red Red Red Red Red
Red Red Red Red Red Red Red Red Red Red Red Red Red
Red Red Red Red Red Red Red Red Red Red Red Red Red
Red Red Red Red Red Red Red Red Red Red Red Red Red
Red Red Red Red Red Red Red Red Red Red Red Red Red
Red Red Red Red Red Red Red Red Red Red Red Red Red
Red Red Red Red Red Red Red Red Red Red Red Red Red
Red Red Red Red Red Red Red Red Red Red Red Red Red
Red Red Red Red Red Red Red Red Red Red Red Red Red
Red Red Red Red Red Red Red Red Red Red Red Red Red
Red Red Red Red Red Red Red Red Red Red Red Red Red
Red Red Red Red Red Red Red Red Red Red Red Red Red
Red Red Red Red Red Red Red Red Red Red Red Red Red
Red Red Red Red Red Red Red Red Red Red Red Red Red
Red Red Red Red Red Red Kelly Sundberg Red Red Red Red
Red Red Red Red Red Red Red Red Red Red Red Red Red
Red Red Red Red Red Red Red Red Red Red Red Red Red
Red Red Red Red Red Red Red Red Red Red Red Red Red

Red Red Red Red Red Red Red Red Red Red Red Red Red
Red Red Red Red Red Red Red Red Red Red Red Red Red
Red Red Red Red Red Red Red Red Red Red Red Red Red
Red Red Red Red Red Red Red Red Red Red Red Red Red
Red Red Red Red Red Red Red Red Red Red Red Red Red
Red Red Red Red Red Red Red Red Red Red Red Red Red
Red Red Red Red Red Red Red Red Red Red Red Red Red
Red Red Red Red Red Red Red Red Red Red Red Red Red
Red Red Red Red Red Red Red Red Red Red Red Red Red

I hope this brings you closure. I hope this brings you closure. I hope this brings you closure. I hope this brings you closure.

Closure is a myth. Closure is just a different kind of opening. There is no way to close something that, once opened, cannot be contained. There is no way to return to the way that things were. I can only ever move forward, and I move forward as a different container. What was inside of me before no longer exists, not even in memory. The only way I can exist is as I am now.

Red is the color of my son sliding onto the delivery room table, slick and warm and crying. Red is the color of my chest after Caleb and I would fuck. Red is the color of my neck after his hands had encircled it. Red is the color of the chunks of hair I found on the floor of my shower when he yanked it out. Red is the color the bruise on my foot turned before it turned purple, then orange, then yellow, and finally, back to red in the form of a star-shaped scar.

Red is me leaving because it wasn't fear that made me leave. It was anger.

The witching hour arrives at night. The witching hour is when it's dark, and I'm alone. Without the distractions of work or school or parenting or friends, I have no psychic protection. The ghosts get in. Their voices taunt me. Now I taunt them back.

No more.

When the witching hour arrives, I run in the darkness until my heart burns, beats red, and obliterates the voices. I light a candle and stare into the red flame—watch it dim and soften. I soften too. My hardness cracks. I call one of my friends and tell them I love them.

I lay out a spread in the tarot. The number nine recurs. Nine is the number of the Hermit. Nine: a period of retreat before completion, before the cycle ends or is born anew. Nine: I have done all that I can for now. In my deck, the Hermit is a turtle who has retreated into its shell. Resting on top of the shell is an oil lamp, and inside of that lamp, a flame burns bright and red.

I hold my star garnet in my hand and stare into its depth. Its red is deep and dark. It is not the red of *stop*. It is the red of *go*.

The Answer Is in the Wound

I'm sorry I make you feel worthless and alone

Every Line Is a Scream

My new therapist asks me why I'm seeing her.

"Because I have PTSD, and I want to be normal again," I say.

She asks what my symptoms are.

"Nightmares."

She asks how often I have nightmares.

"Every night."

She asks what other symptoms I have.

"Insomnia."

"Do you stay awake because you are afraid to fall asleep?" she asks.

"Yes."

She asks what else.

"Dissociation."

She asks how often I'm dissociated.

"Almost all of the time."

"Are you dissociated now?"

"Yes," I say.

My parents have an electric fence around their garden to keep the deer out, but the deer are starving, and once they get into the garden—once they taste a tomato—they will endure the shock of the electric fence again and again to get back to that sweetness. Well-intentioned neighbors feed the deer apples to spare them the fence, but the deer can't digest the sugar, so they starve even more.

In 2018, I published a memoir about why I stayed too long in a violent marriage. I received a six-figure advance, published the book to critical acclaim, and countless women wrote me and told me I changed their lives (men, too, wrote and told me that I changed their lives). Still, nothing changed in *my* life. I was still alone, still angry, still hopeless. I'd thought the book would give me a new life, but I hadn't realized I'd still be the same person. I kept waiting for that alchemy that a book was supposed to bring—the magic of waking up redeemed—but it never happened. Maybe I am too attached to my suffering to be redeemed.

I have never been able to figure out if I write my story or my story writes me because I cannot separate who I am from what has happened to me.

After my husband hit me, his apologies were so sweet. I craved them. A starving woman knows nothing but craving. It was such a self-betrayal to crave momentary satisfaction when the price I'd paid was so terrible, but the craving was so strong.

All things rotting smell sweet as they spoil.

To be redeemed is to be compensated in some way for your suffering or to regain possession of what you had before the suffering. I can never be compensated enough, can never regain what I had before. My heart is inalterably different, and it is a particular kind of heartbreak to realize that wounds can heal without fully closing.

When therapy didn't fix me, I turned to magic. Had my tarot cards read. My astrological chart read. Talked to a clairvoyant. Prayed in a labyrinth in New Mexico. Bought crystals. Smudged sage. I did every white lady witchy appropriation that I could find. I don't know if magic is hope or desperation, but I am desperately hopeful to wake up normal someday.

After my book was published, my ex-husband wrote a public statement and accused me of being the abusive one. He claimed I pulled a knife on him. There was some truth to that. While backed into the corner of our kitchen, I grabbed a large knife and held it to my stomach. I begged him to leave me alone, said I would stab myself if he didn't.

He calmed. "Kelly, give me the knife," he said. I gave him the knife, hand trembling. "You're fucking crazy," he said. "You just pulled a knife on me."

He was right. I was crazy. Still, desperation—fear for one's life—will make one feel crazy, and he was the one who instilled that fear into me.

The day of the Brett Kavanaugh Supreme Court confirmation hearing, I was driving to Indiana to do a reading. I turned on the radio. Christine Blasey Ford, who had accused Kavanaugh of sexual assault, was testifying to her experience. Cory Booker told her he believed her.

"I believe you," he said.

How much power is in those words? So many people didn't believe me. My own parents didn't believe me. I pulled over to the side of the highway and sobbed.

Believe me. Believe me. Believe me.

The next day, a woman came to my reading. Her adult son was getting his pilot's license, and he had to make a certain number of flights, so though it was a short distance, he flew her to Indiana from Illinois. She'd come just to meet me. I knew who she was. We had exchanged emails. Her sister was murdered years before by an abusive husband, and the woman told me that reading my book had helped her understand why her sister loved him.

I never cry at readings. I am highly sophisticated at the art of dissociation. For me, so often, dissociation looks like *nothing*. I can be the most dissociated while performing the best. Maybe this is what domestic violence does—teaches someone how to look completely normal, even while the brain is shut down. A kind of zombification that is both a blessing and a curse. Still, that day, during the Q and A, someone asked me what the hardest part of writing the book was. I said writing about the good moments—the times when he was sweet to me. I started crying, right there in front of everyone. I could see the woman looking at me with tears in her eyes too. She hugged me after the reading, looked at my face for a long time, then told me that I reminded her of her sister. Her son looked at her so tenderly.

Later, I had a drink with my friend Lisa at a dive bar. I wondered what it was about me that reminded the woman of her sister. Lisa said, "She told me what it was. She said that it was because, despite everything you've been through, you are still sweet."

I started crying again, right there in that dive bar in Indiana.

Folks associate the word "triggered" with fragility, and I know that I am not fragile. Survivors of gender violence aren't allowed to get triggered because, when we're triggered, we make other people uncomfortable, and too often, other people's comfort matters more than our suffering. Maybe their discomfort stems from the knowledge that *it could happen to them* too, but when I am overwhelmed and angry or reactive or shut down, I am almost always treated as though I'm insane, even though I am having a completely normal response. In *Healing Trauma*, Peter Levine writes, "Although humans rarely die from trauma, if we do not resolve it, our lives can be severely diminished by its effects. Some people have even described this situation as a 'living death.'" I am one of the *living dead*, yet I am supposed to act normal.

In the time since my book was published, I have been intensely triggered. Writing it, I thought, would be cathartic, and it was, but I am able to see now that I was dissociated during much of its creation. At the end, I was writing in a mania, staying up until 4 a.m., then curling on the floor by my desk and sobbing. I was almost always numb, but at times, the pain would break through. I would gasp at how much it hurt; still, the pain was such sweet relief. Numbness, too, is a burden, and I would rather feel.

No, I'd rather be numb.
No, I'd rather feel.
No, I'd rather be numb.

The emotional alchemist asks me what is going on in my life. I tell her that I have broken up with a man I have been sleeping with—that I wanted a relationship, but he didn't want that label with me. She asks what would have been different with the label. I have to concede that nothing would have been different, that I already got as much as I wanted from him. She tells me that maybe I am too attached to labels, and I wonder if she's right.

The emotional alchemist taps into energy and shifts emotions; she alchemizes feelings, and I cannot possibly explain what that means. I have a PhD, and I am aware of how irrational this sounds. There is no amount of convincing I can offer to make this process sound real, but I feel the shift—the alchemy—and she knows things that I am incapable of telling her because I don't even know them myself. She roots around in there—in my psyche—feels for what is broken. This time, it is abandonment. She says the word "abandonment" when she finds it. I start crying again; I am always crying.

Abandonment. Abandonment. Abandonment.

I left him, but my ex-husband abandoned me long before I ran out the door with nothing but a suitcase and a duffle bag full of our child's LEGOs.

When they didn't believe me, my parents abandoned me too.

The first time the emotional alchemist rooted around in my psyche, she found horror. Her voice quieted. "It's horror," she said with respect and reverence and concern. An entire genre of film is rooted around the concept. The women are always screaming.

Horror. Horror. Horror.

I will never again be a woman who hasn't held a knife to her own stomach in order to save her life.

The man I broke up with because he didn't want a relationship with me is kind. He is younger than me, and he wants a life that looks different than mine. Rationally, I know I want a life that looks different than his too, but in the meantime, we have been good to each other. No one has ever touched me with such gentleness. The last time we had sex, I wept afterward. I tried to explain it to him. "To be touched with gentleness after having been touched with so much violence makes me feel raw." He looked sad for me, and that made me feel sad for myself. Sometimes I forget that my experience wasn't typical. I didn't know how much I craved gentle touch. A starving woman only knows craving.

My abusive ex-husband is, by all accounts, happily remarried and has two new babies. I am still alone.

This is a peculiar form of gaslighting.

☼ ☼ ☼

Just after I defended my dissertation, and before my book was published, I impulsively got a tattoo. It was no fault of the tattoo artist, but the new ink was not what I wanted. Then my book was published. My book was born during the period of #MeToo, which meant it was born into a world of collective trauma that mimicked and reflected my personal trauma. I wanted to start over on my own terms, wanted to start with a cover-up of the tattoo. I messaged a tattoo artist, Kat, whose work I admired. I told her my story and asked for her help. I sent her my writing. She wrote back that she didn't usually take cover-ups, but she also didn't close the door entirely. I was persistent and gave her total artistic freedom with no size constraints. I knew, somehow, that I needed this, and that I needed it to be from her.

The emotional alchemist asks me to give myself permission to feel worthy of being loved. She asks me to say this out loud. I cannot. My voice stops in my throat. Instead, I say, "This is very hard for me."

"I know it is," she says, "but you need to say it."

"I give myself permission to feel worthy of being loved," I say. I am crying again.

In Kat's studio, she approached me with her design. It was stunning. She had meditated on my story while she drafted this large-scale, minimalist tattoo. There is an all-knowing eye in the middle for wisdom and protection flanked by the figure of a guardian angel with wings. On each of the wings are circles that symbolize giving and receiving.

Palo Santo and a Dark Moon Intention candle burned on a small table beside her. She asked me to lean forward, and the needle entered my skin. She was gentle, would stop regularly and wipe the blood with a damp paper towel. The coolness of the towel offered such relief on my burning skin. We worked for seven hours. She told me that my left side is receiving, and my right side is giving. I felt more pain on the right side, pulled away from her in those moments. I have a very hard time giving—or trusting—or loving.

When the needle hit the same point on my spine where my ex-husband's fist once slammed, I began to quietly sob. Kat said nothing, just offered me a tissue. I remembered his fist, remembered the crack, the shock, the pain. I felt it all again in the needle, and I sobbed. I was in my body. Present. There was no dissociation, and though it hurt, I felt free.

Though I was sobbing on the outside, I was screaming on the inside. I pictured him standing in front of me, and I screamed.

You stole my life from me. You stole my life from me. You stole my life from me.

The needle traced lines where his fists had once created bruises. Every line was a scream. Every line of my book, too, was a scream. All this time, I thought that I had been crying, but I was screaming.

Believe me. Believe me. Believe me.
Abandonment. Abandonment. Abandonment.
Horror. Horror. Horror.

* * *

I didn't tell my parents about the tattoo. Didn't want to risk their judgment, but this past summer, I spent Father's Day with them in Idaho. There is so much regret in my father's eyes; he believes me now. My mother and I sat in a hot spring, and she saw the tattoo. She didn't judge. We have had to learn how to love each other despite this history between us.

"It's a guardian angel," I said.

I hadn't had a guardian angel when I needed one.

As my mother and I sat in that spring and stared into the mountains where I had backpacked with my father so many times before, I remembered seeing a deer a couple of summers earlier. A doe. She stopped and looked at me. She was plump, definitely not starving.

I whispered "goodbye" to her when she left.

As we neared the end of the tattoo, Kat told me, "I know exactly when it's going to hurt, and you are going to feel it emotionally, but I will get you through it."

When that time came, she said, "It's going to hurt, and I need you to lean into it. Let whatever comes out come out."

It did hurt, but I leaned into the pain in the way that turns hurt into such exquisite pleasure. This is the life I'm left with. There is nothing that can be done now. I heard Kat crying softly behind me. It was painful and terrible and beautiful.

Ritchie County Mall

Caleb and I are driving from Morgantown to Parkersburg in West Virginia to see his parents. "Can we stop for a bathroom break?" I ask.

He pulls into a 7-Eleven. "Welcome to the Ritchie County Mall," he says.

"The what?" I ask.

"The Ritchie County Mall. We call it that because there's nothing else in Ritchie County," he says. I laugh. No one can make me laugh like Caleb.

I look back at Reed in his car seat. He smiles, his Curious George stuffed toy gripped in his arms. Reed has always been a happy travel companion—rarely fussy or difficult on long drives. He was born on the full moon and is the only child I'll ever have. My moon baby.

"I'll be back," I say to Caleb, as I open the door.

"I know you will," Caleb says, smiling.

Breathe deeply in a West Virginia forest, and the thick air has a distinctive taste. Just like it looks. Rich and fertile. Ritchie County is no different. The hardwood forests tight and luscious. Large swaths of dirt roads slice through the greenery and lead to cavernous holes with tall gray injection wells jutting out of them. Light changes around the injection wells—becomes a faint pall that never stops shining, even on the darkest nights.

I pull into the Ritchie County Mall, then park next to the red Toyota that Caleb and I bought together years earlier. I look down at my phone, at the car on the other side of me, at the ice machine in front of me. Anywhere but at Caleb.

The car door opens behind me, and seven-year-old Reed slides into his seat and buckles his seatbelt. "Did you have a good weekend?" I ask.

"It was okay," Reed says. We pull out of the parking lot behind Caleb, then Caleb turns left, and we turn right.

The Ritchie County Mall is the halfway point between Athens, Ohio, where I have moved with Reed so I can get my PhD, and Morgantown, West Virginia, where Caleb stayed after our divorce in the house we once owned together. I think of myself—always driving halfway back to home—but never arriving.

I'm at the Ritchie County Mall waiting when Caleb pulls up alongside me. Reed is eight and slides into the car. "I haven't eaten," he says. I turn off the car, take him inside, and ask for a piece of pizza. I order myself a chicken jalapeno taquito. An impulse snack I know I'll regret. The woman puts gloves on, then scoops them both into paper dishes. In the car, Reed and I eat. "How is your pizza?" I ask.

"Not great," he says. I eat my taquito. It is also not great. As we near Parkersburg, Caleb's hometown, I think of Caleb's family. We drive by the turn-off to his sister's house. She was once my sister too. Heartburn settles into my chest. It distracts me from the heartache. Heartache, too, is a physical pain.

My anger is made of pain and hurt and want. It feels bottomless sometimes.

Caleb's sister meets me at the Ritchie County Mall instead of Caleb. She and I used to get wine drunk after the kids went to sleep and tell each other how much we loved each other. "I always wanted a sister," I would say.

"I can't imagine Caleb with anyone but you," she would say.

Her children loved me too. The daughter always chose to sit next to me on family outings, but I secretly preferred the son, who was impulsive but goodhearted. I recognized myself in him. I used to comfort him in secret when he was in trouble. Once, his father made him sit inside the house alone while the rest of us played football outside, and I snuck in and held him while he cried on the couch. "You're a good boy," I said.

I remember this, as my sister-in-law waves at me from her minivan.

Reed gets out of the car, and I put it into reverse, but then hear a knock at my window. I look over, startled. My former niece and nephew are standing outside the window, waving and smiling at me. I open the door and give them both long hugs. I know the family is not supposed to speak to me. It is a generosity that despite this, she lets the kids see me. I smile at her. She smiles back as Reed gets into her minivan to leave with her.

On the drive home, I cry deep sobs that come from my stomach. When I get home, I email her. "Thank you for being nice to me," I say.

She emails back, "I will always be nice to you."

A friend later says to me, "A sister is always the first to know her brother's violence."

I am trying to write a piece that isn't about how Caleb used to hit me. I am tired of being *that woman*. I am so much more than that. I am a mother, a writer, a very good friend to those I love. I am funny and happy and accomplished. I am not just "that woman who was abused."

Still, I can no longer write my story, any part of it, without at least some of it coming back to the reality that I am also "that woman who was abused."

When you leave a man who abuses you, you must leave everything that is his. Sometimes that means leaving your sister and niece and nephew who, it turns out, were never really yours to begin with.

Diesel trucks idle outside the Ritchie County Mall. I have dropped Reed off, just as busses full of oil-rig workers have arrived. Men in boots covered with thick red clay swarm into the building to get their nightly beer or hot dog. I am inside to buy a snack. "Are you from around here?" The question comes from a man holding a twenty-four-ounce Budweiser Straw-Ber-Rita, four bottles of Boone's Farm, and a big plastic cup full of ice with a straw. I shake my head no. "Have you ever seen so much pipeline activity?" he asks. Again, I shake my head no. He tells me that he used to be on welfare, but now makes $2,200 a week. He says this with both gratitude and desperation.

I'm anti-fracking, but I'm also poor, and something in me sparks at that number—$2,200 a week. That's almost twice what I make in a month. I'm supporting Reed with student loans I may never be able to pay back. I know the way that poverty erodes the soul. I have felt that hunger. I smile at him. "That's great," I say.

"Drill, baby, drill!" he says.

When I get in my car, "Lost Cause" by Beck is playing on my stereo as I drive home to spend another Friday evening alone.

When Caleb and I divorced, splitting our assets was easy because we had so few of them. Splitting the debts was the harder part because we had plenty of those, and I ended up with most of them. This is what happens to women financially in divorce; we lose.

Caleb and I had a giant sectional couch we financed for $25 a month for five years. It was in Caleb's name, and he wanted to keep it, but I took it because he had everything else. He had to continue paying on it for a few years after the divorce, and I knew that he must have been angry as I cuddled up on it next to our son.

I realized one Friday night, after I'd returned home alone and sat on my spot on the couch—the most uncomfortable spot made even more so by the sagging that my refusal to sit anywhere else had caused—that I had chosen that spot because it was the only part of the couch where Caleb and I had never cuddled, had never lain entwined together. I was trying to avoid the ghost of those memories. Always, the ghosts haunt me.

It wasn't just the couch. Everything in that marriage was on credit. Every embrace—every moment of tenderness—was a debt that would have to be repaid.

Grief was the interest.

I'm shoveling a handful of peanuts into my mouth in my car at the Ritchie County Mall when Caleb pulls in next to me. I look over, and there is a woman sitting in the passenger seat. Younger than me. Blonde. Cute. I don't know what to do, so I wave at her. Her mouth opens in surprise, gapes, then she glares at me. She pointedly looks away, but looks back, glares even more. She has clearly prepared for this moment.

No one has ever looked at me like that before. It makes me feel wretched. I am not used to being disliked, but I can only imagine what he must have told her.

As I drive away, I text him and ask him not to bring her on the handoffs, say that they are already hard enough for everyone, and that it doesn't help that she was rude to me. This obviously brings him satisfaction. He texts back that he'll do what he wants, says that she, too, will do what she wants. Anger spikes in me, and then, I do something I know I'll regret.

I text back, "I'm prettier than her."

I want to say I'm not the kind of woman to do something like that, but I *did* do something like that. Apparently, I am the kind of woman to do something like that and then feel shame about it.

I am not prettier than her.

※ ※ ※

Reed and I leave the Ritchie County Mall on a dark Sunday night after Caleb has dropped him off. I ask him about his weekend. He says to me, "I can't tell if Dad has too much temper, or if you just take things more lightly than most people," then, "Dad's girlfriend is calm. She doesn't have a short temper. She is a lot like you, Mom."

I listen first, then ask the obvious question, "Does your father hurt you?" I know that, if it's not physical, there is little I can do in West Virginia family courts.

He responds, "Dad yells at me almost every weekend now. The only times he doesn't yell at me are when other people are around." He pauses, then says, "I don't think Dad's girlfriend thinks his yelling is okay, but she is afraid to say anything, or he will yell at her too." Then he says what I have always feared he would say: "I think I bring it on myself. I am like my dad. I have a short temper. I know that Dad can't change, but do you think *I* can change?"

Finally, he asks me, "Where do you think my dad's temper came from?"

I don't know how to answer my son's question. I have already driven myself mad trying to find an answer. All I know is that Caleb's rage is a rhizome. It grows continuously outward. It sprouts new shoots and roots at intervals. It is impossible to identify the first root.

I am not the root, and Reed is not the root.

I tell him, "You are worthy of love. You can live in a calm home. I know this because you live in one with me. You do not deserve what is happening to you." I ask him, "Do you want me to talk to your father about the yelling?"

Reed says, "No, because then he would just yell at you. I think the only thing I can do is learn to take it."

I don't know what to say then because there is truth to what he says, so I simply say, "I'm sorry, honey." He sniffles in the dark backseat.

When we get home, I hug him in the hallway, and I say, "I want you to know that your father's anger is not your fault, and you do not deserve it." His little boy's body eases into my chest, and he lets me hold him for a long time. The entire time I am holding him, I am thinking, *Just collapse yourself into my love, and don't think of anything else. Just think of this: Think of how worthy you are. Think of how loved you are. Think of how you are not your father. Think of how your father is not your destiny.*

Caleb's girlfriend becomes Reed's stepmother. They have a wedding on Caleb's family's farm with wildflowers. I find the photos online. She looks beautiful. Caleb looks ridiculous in a straw hat, mountain man beard, and vest. He has doubled down on his "Appalachian Americana" ethos. But Reed looks so adorable in between them. He wears a green plaid shirt, and though he hates having his picture taken, he's smiling. He's happy. He looks like a part of their family. I only ever want for him to be happy, so I am surprised by the feelings that arise when I look at the photos. Deep tenderness that Reed is cared for. Rage at how smug Caleb looks. And jealousy that his bride is seemingly living the life I wanted.

When I left Caleb, no one told me how long it takes to heal from a particular kind of violence that is borne from love, that I would never—to this day—believe that he didn't love me. Only that he didn't know *how* to love. Still, I tell myself that his love must be enough for this new woman, so what is wrong with me?

I cannot tell you how long it takes to heal from violence that is borne from love because I have not healed yet.

Reed is ten when he gets into the car at the Ritchie County Mall and pulls out the dinner that his dad packed for him. A sandwich, apple, and homemade cookies. "Oh, did your stepmom make you cookies?" I ask.
"Yes," he says. "But I'm not allowed to share them with you."

When I left Caleb, no one told me he would remain unscathed, that the only people who would be damaged by his abuse would be Reed and me.

I pick Reed up at the Ritchie County Mall, and he chats the entire way home. He's eleven, and he tells me about his little sister, and how they tried to feed her mashed carrots for the first time. He tells me how she can now reach out and grab things. He tells me he had homemade cheeseburgers for dinner, made by his dad. He tells me that he, his dad, and his stepmom have been watching *Stranger Things* at lunchtime, but they watched *The Simpsons* at dinnertime for comic relief. He tells me about his birthday party next weekend where he is going to watch *Thor* with his dad and a couple of his friends. He tells me all kinds of things about various Marvel characters that I have no interest in. He is happy. He had a good weekend with his dad. I needed a break from Reed, but it turns out that he needed a break from me too. This should be okay. It *is* okay.

A child's happiness should be enough to make the mother happy, but still, I am filled with longing, and loss, and loneliness.

"I'm glad you had a good weekend, baby," I say. He still lets me call him baby.

He looks at me for a long time. "I missed you," he says.

I don't have to drive to the Ritchie County Mall on this Friday because it is Reed's sixth grade graduation. Caleb attends with his wife, who looks delicate and kind as she holds their chubby baby, as well as his parents—Mimi and Papaw to Reed. I have still never been introduced to Reed's stepmom. I asked for it once, and Caleb texted back (we only communicate via text), "She will never shake your hand."

I have prepared for this—knew I wouldn't want to be alone—so I attend with my friend who wears fishnets and says explicitly that she wants "to make Caleb feel weird." If Caleb has doubled down on his Appalachian Americana ethos, then I have doubled down on my "feminist single mom with a PhD" ethos. Maybe we are trying to distinguish ourselves from each other, or maybe we are both finally able to be who we wanted to be all along. All I know is that we can't be in a gymnasium and sit on the same side.

The principal gives a speech and asks us to recognize all of the parents who have been doing the work, showing up to conferences and all of the school events. I try not to, but I start crying because I have done it all by myself, and I am tired.

Caleb's mom, a former elementary school teacher, has snuck to the front to take a photo, and while she is hustling back to her seat, she sees my tears and stops. She smiles gently at me and waves. I cry more. I know that they know what he did.

In a West Virginia forest in summer, the sunlight filters through the leaves in patterns that look like stars. At night, the leaves feel like stars, and the stars feel like leaves. It is all inescapably beautiful. Still, winter is like the pall left from the injection wells—bare and lonely and hard. The contrast is dizzying. Caleb is not West Virginia, but he could be. His turns so sudden.

I had a very involved dream recently that I was trying to untangle two pieces of string, but they just kept getting caught up into a larger ball. As hard as I try, I cannot unravel what happened to me. I cannot make it make sense. All of this love that I have is such a mess. In my story, Caleb is an injection well, and I am the pall that surrounds it.

But that isn't the real story. Even the stories we tell ourselves can be fictions. I know this because, when I step back from all of the hurt and loss and look at my story with a wider lens, I can see what was obscured all of those evenings spent at the Ritchie County Mall. That it would get better. That I would get a job—a real job—a tenure-track job, and I would start paying a former student to drive Reed to West Virginia every other weekend because Reed liked the student, and I had done my time on that road. That Reed and I would grow closer and closer as the years unfolded, and he would joke that he was someday going to write a memoir about having to spend his childhood divided between his "feminist hippy mom and hillbilly dad." That we were good at laughing together, even when things were hard. That I may never be able to unravel what happened, but Caleb no longer owns me, and that is all that matters now. That, for so many years, I was driving halfway toward home, but then home changed. Home became this boy and me together. Just us. A mother and her child who was born under a full moon. That the moon sometimes obscures the stars, but it doesn't mean they're gone. That the stars would spin out in unexpected ways. That the leaves in Ohio would look just like the leaves in West Virginia, but there would be safety in them. That the loss would no longer feel so acute. It would feel more like possibility. More like an entire solar system. That I would learn how to reframe what "healing" meant to me—that it was okay to not be healed as long as I was healing.

Couplet

When I carried my son in my womb, it was just the two of us—my heartbeat a constant echo in his darkness, and his heartbeat an echo in mine. When I birthed him onto the table in a hot, bloody mess, it was still just the two of us, bound together by that slippery thread.

When his father cut the cord, I did not feel the severing, but I felt the absence.

I missed my child, even though he was in my arms feeding at my breast with the hunger of someone who had been starving.

How does a mother miss a baby while he is feeding at her breast?

In the same way that she misses an older child while he is at his father's house—with a kind of longing for something that never existed.

My son gazes out our sliding glass doors at two chairs on the patio, nestled next to each other.

"Who was here?" he asks.

* * *

"A friend," I say.

I hadn't moved the chairs when my friend left and my son returned, preferring instead to be reminded of the kind of intimacy that I hadn't experienced in years.

We—my friend and I—had sat in those chairs next to each other and gazed at the full moon the night before.

We were lovers but not yet in love.

A different friend said that the French use the word "lover" in ways that we Americans don't.

According to her, a lover can be someone with whom you share an intimacy but not a commitment—more than a friend but less than a partner—and not, as we Americans so crudely call it, a "fuck-buddy."

When I left my marriage, I cried to another friend that I hadn't wanted to parent on my own, that I wanted to be a family.

"Two is still a family," she told me.

Two is the smallest possible family.

We are a family, my son and I.

When I left my marriage and made a family of two, there was no room in our little family for anyone else—my son had to be the entirety of my universe.

When I left my marriage and made a family of two, I chose to place my son's needs over my own desires.

* * *

Is there a word for a part-time mother?
An all-but-every-other-weekend mother?

I told my lover, "I didn't want children because I knew that, if I had them, I'd have to get my life together and be a good mother."
I told my lover, "I am a good mother, but it has not come without a cost."

Needs, desires, needs, desires, needs, desires, needs, desires.
My child needs things that I do not desire.

I am a mother now.
Now I am not a mother.

Now I am not a mother.
I am a mother now.

I can no longer relate to partnered mothers.
You have no idea what it feels like to do it alone, I think.

I'd still rather do it alone.
In my life, one wasn't the loneliest number; three was.

If I'm honest with myself, the times when I am *not a mother now* are some of my happiest.
But everything that makes me happy also brings me sorrow now.

* * *

You and me.
   Me and you.

Me and you.
   You and me.

Which comes first?
   The *me* or the *you*?

You, you, you, you, you, you, you, you, you, you, you, you, you, you, you, you, you.
   Me.

When my son and I became the smallest possible family, it became *just the two of us* again, and that felt right, except for when he was gone, and it was only me.
   I never learned how to fill the absence—not on the day that my son was born, or the day that I watched him walk into the doors of his kindergarten, or the day that I picked him up from school and said, "We're not going home to Daddy tonight."

"I know," he said.
   He was seven.

I have dreams for my son.
   I had dreams for myself.

* * *

What are dreams if not wishes made to the universe?

What are wishes if not dreams unfulfilled?

"I used to think I wanted a stepdad," my son says to me, "but I don't think that I do anymore because now I think that would ruin our dynamic."

"You're in luck," I say, "because it's just the two of us."

I do not tell him that I have a lover, an every-other-weekend lover who is not quite a friend and not quite a partner.

I do not tell him that I have missed being held at night.

"I don't think it's your son that you're worried about," my therapist says.

"I think you're worried about yourself and how it will feel if you introduce your son to a man who turns around and hurts you."

I do not tell my son when my lover turns into a partner.

I want to let the relationship grow, I tell myself, though I fear that my heart is infertile.

When I finally tell my son about the person who went from being a friend to lover to partner, I say, "I want you to know that you are always my first priority."

"It never occurred to me that I wasn't," he says.

The loneliness of a single mother is a deep, dark river.

The current so strong, so erosive, to everything that might otherwise grow.

* * *

I am a mother now.
    Now I am not a mother.

Now I am not a mother.
    I am a mother now.

My son is only a few years away from leaving my home to make his own.
    It is not lost on me that, though two is lonely, one is still lonelier.

There is a tension in the wanting of parenting alone.
    The wanting of solitude, the wanting of companionship, the wanting of solitude, the wanting of companionship, the wanting of solitude, the wanting of companionship.

My lover calms me in ways that my son should not and cannot.
    My lover slows the current, but the river still unfurls in a deep, dark ribbon ahead of me.

You and you and me.
    Me and you and you.

Me and you and you.
    You and you and me.

Which comes first?
    The *me* or the *you* or the *you*?

* * *

Me, me, me, me, me, me, me, me, me, me, me, me, me, me, me, me, me, me, me, me, me.

You.

Oh, my son, I want you to have everything.

I want you to be loved, I want you to be safe, I want you to have a life with little suffering, and I want you to love a partner who doesn't break you.

Most of all, I do not want your heartbeat to echo this darkness of mine.

My son, I do not want you to drown in my loneliness.

I know that I can only give you some—but not all—of these wants.

My son, do not be swept away into that dark current.

Sometimes I sit in one of those patio chairs, stare at the sky, and think of my son asking so thoughtfully, "Who was here?"

I should have answered that *I was*.

Because it is always me—alone—in every moment.

I alone gaze at the full moon, I alone leave my marriage, I alone tell my seven-year-old that we aren't going home to Daddy, I alone grieve every other weekend, I alone love every other weekend, and I alone wade into that dark river.

* * *

Here is how to be alone.
   Be alone.

My son, you cannot drown in my river if you do not wade into it.
   My son, your life is your own.

My Mother, My Self, and I

Reed and I are on the couch eating pizza and watching the movie *Lady Bird*. He's fourteen, and this would not be his preferred choice of movie, but we're quarantining during the pandemic, and we've come to an agreement that we will watch "his" movie one night, then "mine" the next. While quarantining, we've spent our days in different rooms on our laptops, then come together in the evenings to eat and watch television. We've always been close, but neither of us has been in a room with another person for months, and this has created a closeness that feels unusual for a mother and her teenage son, though I have no idea what *usual* looks like because he is, and will be, the only child I ever raise.

Lady Bird, as a character, is annoying but endearing. Idealistic but earnest. She does and says dumb things. She embarrasses herself constantly. She pushes back on her mother's boundaries in ways that feel both necessary and, often, unkind. Her mother, Marion, is critical and pragmatic to a fault. She yells at Lady Bird a lot, and Lady Bird yells back. Marion thinks Lady Bird's ambitions are frivolous and actively tries to stifle them. Neither character is very likable, but by the end of the film, the viewer realizes they are both flawed. They love each other deeply, but Marion, in particular, only knows how to love via control. As the movie nears its end, Reed turns to me and says with a completely straight face, "Do you like this movie because it's about you and Grandma?"

As a kid, I'd fantasized that there were two versions of my mother. There was the nice mother who lived in the world with me, and in the coat closet, there was a secret mother—a cruel Russian spy (this was the 1980s during the Cold War)—who hid and waited for her chance to come out and abuse me. I was an imaginative child, but I didn't actually believe this to be true. The fantasy brought me comfort because I was too young to reckon with the reality that my mother could be both things at once—the loving, kind mother who provided for me so well, and the cruel, mercurial mother who seemed to resent me for being alive.

When I was twenty-two and dating my first boyfriend—a man much older than me who had a master's degree in "psychoanalysis," as he liked to call it—I told him that story. My boyfriend, in a manner that was typical of him, tried to use this to diagnose me. I can't remember what the diagnosis was this time, only that he insisted I had genuinely believed I had two mothers, and that indicated I had a fractured psyche. He was probably correct that I had a fractured psyche, but I had always known I only had one mother. Knowing I only had one mother was why the story was sad.

That boyfriend wasn't the only man to try and diagnose me. My ex-husband tried to diagnose me too. He claimed I had borderline personality disorder (BPD)—that his therapist (who had never met me) had offered the diagnosis. My ex-husband claimed it was my disorder that had provoked him to abuse me. I brought this up with my therapist at the time, and we talked for a while before she realized I believed him. She said, "Kelly, I didn't think I needed to say this, but you do not have borderline personality disorder. If you did, that would be something we could work on, but you don't. I need you to know that."

Still, for years after that, as I struggled with friendships and close relationships, I secretly feared he had been right about me. Post-abuse, I was so reactive that my boundaries had become like an electric fence, and I didn't know how much PTSD and BPD could look like each other. I had realized by then, though, that abusive people will weaponize diagnoses against their victims, that weaponizing diagnoses is part of the pattern. In the years that followed, I learned how much BPD was the most weaponized and unfairly stigmatized diagnosis in our culture, even though it, too, was a trauma response.

The reality when I was struggling with close relationships was that some of my bad behavior was because of my trauma, some of my bad behavior was because of my poorly executed boundaries, and some of my bad behavior was because I was being a shitty person. If a friend didn't reach out for a while, I'd text them that they obviously didn't want to be my friend. If someone else hurt my feelings, I wouldn't say anything in the moment, but would later write a long, angry email. A friend once told me that a guy from a graduate workshop had called me "the perfect victim," and in the next moment, I messaged him, "Fuck you. How is that for the perfect victim?" To be fair, that guy was a jerk, but I wasn't helping my cause. I wanted so deeply to be loved for who I was, but I was irrational and erratic. Who would love me that way?

I could be pathologized to a degree, but pathology wasn't the entire answer. I also just had some bad qualities. Let me rephrase that, I *have* some bad qualities. I can be self-absorbed, prickly, and even downright mean. I've lost people I've loved because of these qualities, which I regret deeply, so I've worked hard to overcome them. A huge part of that work has been holding myself accountable, while trying not to hate myself because I've had enough therapy to know that hating myself won't make me a better person.

A few years ago, my mother said to me, "Your father and I want to pay for your therapy. We don't want you to miss therapy because you can't afford it." It turns out my mother had started getting therapy, and she finally understood the importance of it. I had wondered about that. There had been signs. Big signs. She'd been offering more encouragement when it came to my career, had helped financially when I needed it, had watched my son so I could travel and go to writer's residencies. And the last time I'd visited my parents in Idaho, my mother hadn't said anything about my weight, even though I had clearly gained. In the past, she would have said, "It looks like someone has stopped working out," or "You shouldn't wear shirts that stick to your belly. They're not flattering." This time, though, she hadn't criticized my outfits. Hadn't second-guessed my judgment or life choices. I actually had a good time there.

At the dinner table one night, my mother was telling a story and said, "I don't judge people, but . . ."

I interrupted her, "Mom, I have heard you judge *a lot* of people."

Reed and my father laughed, but then Reed looked at me like I was in trouble because my mother didn't like being teased. But this time, my mother laughed too. She shook her head and said, "Well, I try not to be like that anymore."

I knew my mother had lost friendships over the years too. She hadn't told me about them, but I'd noticed when the friends disappeared. My mother and I were similar in that our friendships were very important to us, and we are similar in that we have many very good and longstanding friendships, but we've both lost friends too. Years ago, I lost my very best friend. I know it was my fault, and I live with a lot of regret about that. I know my mom had a similar friendship, and when I see that friend in my hometown, she always hugs me and asks how I am, but she never asks about my mother.

Shortly before the pandemic, Reed and I moved to Columbus, Ohio. Because of the divorce, we had moved a lot, and Reed was worried about being the new kid again. I worried about him too. I called a psychic who a friend had recommended, and I asked her if he would be okay. She said that he would, that he is "accidentally popular" everywhere he goes, and that he would thrive. She suggested that he might be in school online for a while, which I scoffed at because, at that time, there were no indications (to the non-psychics at least) that a global pandemic was around the corner. She told me that I was a good mother, that I had done right by him, and I started to bawl because, ever since he was born, all I have wanted was to be a better mother to him than my mother was to me.

My feelings about my mother were so mixed up. She had been, at times, both emotionally and physically abusive, but she had also always been there for me when I needed her. In fact, there were times when I felt that she liked it if my life was in crisis because those were the times when she was at her best. My therapist told me it was okay to feel mixed up—that inconsistency is its own kind of discomfort—that if my mother had been consistently abusive, that might have actually been easier.

I went into parenting Reed with a determination to always be my very best self for him, and I think I can honestly say that, despite my bad qualities, ever since the divorce, I've been a good mother to Reed. I've been there for him. I've never been mean or abusive to him. I've been consistent and stable. I can also say honestly that I couldn't have been that mother within the context of my abusive marriage, that I was not as good of a mother when I was married. I was too consumed with trying to survive to be a good mother.

I don't know what my mother might have been trying to survive when I was a child, but I know she'd been an orphan when she was a child. She'd been raised by her grandmother, and then her older brother. She'd had no parenting models to follow. When I was a child, my mother worked a stressful job as a registered nurse with twelve-hour days that began at 3 a.m. My parents are happy now, but when I was a child, they fought a lot. My father was a kind man, but he was not the most attentive or involved, and divorce, to my mother, would not have been an option. My hometown was also predominantly Mormon, so my mother felt that she didn't fit in. She often felt alone.

The psychic was blunt with me. She told me that my mother's kinds of narcissisms (not in the diagnosable sense) were in me too. That my mother's feral qualities live in me, but those qualities are also what saved me. She said that I have tried to talk myself out of being feral, but the feral part is my divine feminine. My rage is my power.

I think of sending that "Fuck you" to the guy from my graduate workshop. It was a moment where I felt completely feral, overtaken by rage, and yes, I acted impulsively and irrationally, but I also didn't listen to what he was saying. I didn't let the words "perfect victim" into my heart, where they would quietly poison me. There should have been a middle ground between rage and self-hatred, but at that time in my life, I didn't have the skills to find middle ground. The choice was between rage and self-hatred, and I made the choice that was necessary for my survival.

Like me, my mother survived terrible things. I will never know the full extent of what she survived, but she saved herself. In the process of saving herself, she wasn't always the best mother, but she tried, and though she did so much wrong, she also did a lot right. The only reason I was able to save myself was because of my mother's fierce strength. The only reason I have been able to be a better parent to Reed is because, though she wasn't always consistent, ultimately, she showed me how to parent well.

At the end of *Lady Bird*, Marion says to Lady Bird, "I want you to be the very best version of yourself that you can be." It's such a poignant moment and recognizes Lady Bird as an individual who is separate from her mother. We can all only be the very best versions of ourselves. I have, at times, been the very worst version of myself, but as a mother, I believe I am the best version of myself, and when I look at my mother, who is now in her seventies, I see a mother who is the very best version of herself too. It is such a rare gift to observe a parent become the version of themselves that you, the child, always needed. I no longer have an evil mother hiding in a closet. There is only the mother who saved herself. The mother who saved me. The mother who gave me the strength to save my own child.

Everything That Brings Me Joy Also Brings Me Sorrow Now

My therapist Liz says, "You're going to need to find something spiritual to fill the holes." My spirit has so many holes in it that all of the love just falls right through. Where my love goes, I don't know. Some of it is trapped in my abuser's fists. There is a part of me that will always love him. I have tried to excise it. A reiki healer says that, when she held her hands over my abdomen, she felt the spectre of him. She heard the words "Just in case," and she told me I need to cut the cord, but I have tried. The cord remains tethered to me in some inexplicable fashion. I am now in love with a man who is nothing like my ex but who has hurt me still. On my drive home, I hear the words *just in case just in case just in case just in case just in case*. There is no part of me that wants to be with my ex in this lifetime, but maybe my spirit is holding out for a different lifetime? How could I even want that? *I don't know I don't know I don't know I don't know I don't know I don't know I don't know I don't know.*

I call my lover from the car and break up with him because I cannot break up with myself. He accepts it; he knows he has hurt me very badly. We sleep in the same bed that night, but early in the morning, I embrace him from behind. I feel his body relax. He is confused. Of course he is. In the morning, while he is eating his breakfast, I tell him I don't want to break up. Still, staying together is so painful. I wanted a lover who would never hurt me, but that lover didn't exist, couldn't exist. I only know how to love through hurting. My lover has done nothing that is unforgivable, but the same part of my soul that says *just in case* about my ex rebukes me for my forgiveness; it is the part of me that is supremely fucked. Wasn't I too forgiving with my ex? Didn't my forgiveness create this trauma? *My forgiveness is the problem my forgiveness is the problem my forgiveness is the problem my forgiveness is the problem.* Judith Herman writes in *Trauma and Recovery,* "Over time as most people fail the survivor's exacting test of trustworthiness, she tends to withdraw from relationships. The isolation of the survivor thus persists even after she is free." I am free, and yet still so alone.

In *Waking the Tiger,* Peter Levine writes that shamanistic cultures believe that trauma separates the soul from the body. "Missing important parts of their souls, people become lost in states of spiritual suspension," he claims. He likens this to what Mircea Eliade calls "rape of the soul." My soul has been raped. My soul is lost. My soul wanders in darkness. My brain and heart are still with me. My brain and heart want to forgive my lover, but my soul is wailing alone that she can *never again.* I visit psychics, and alchemists, and reiki healers in the hopes that one of them will be able to corral my soul for me, to return her to where she belongs. They come close.

Closer, probably, than my therapist has. My soul does not want to be found though.

My lover sees my soul. I know this. He sees her, and he isn't scared of her. He doesn't try to push her or change her or trap her. He's patient.

If I don't find something spiritual—meaningful—contained within my trauma, then what am I left with? An empty soul? I do not believe in soulmates, but I'm taking my chances because I know I can never have one if my soul is lost. And what is a soul? Some ineffable goodness? I fully believe that my soul brought my lover and his sweetness to me. I also believe my soul will keep him from me. I have to tell her to stand down. Maybe I can't will away the darkness because it's the only place where I can find her, so I sink myself so deep into it, so deep that I might drown but I don't. In *Bluets*, Maggie Nelson writes, "Mostly I have felt myself becoming a servant of sadness. I am still looking for the beauty in that." I, too, am a servant of sadness. *I am a servant of sadness I am a servant of sadness I am a servant of sadness I am a servant of sadness I am a servant of sadness.* My lover, too, becomes a servant of my sadness. It is unavoidable. He is a willing servant, though not a supplicant, and together, we hold this sadness. We hold his too. Then, finally, something happens.

Trust needs time. Trust cannot be hurried, and as the years pass, I begin to trust myself. It's not that I surface. It's not that I will ever again be in possession of my soul from the *before*.

It's not that I find light at the end of the darkness. It's that I learn how to make a home inside of the darkness. It's that I look at those who came before me—so many—and think that I, too, can bloom under a shadow. It's that I look at my lover standing beside me, a generous and gracious servant of my sadness, *and I can find the beauty in that.* It's that regardless of what I become, shadow or not, lover or not, I am not defined by my darkness. I will always be defined by my light. All along, the light was where my love landed. The light was always there, and it always will be.

PART 5

AFTER

Gifts

A while ago, I sat on a deck in the Idaho sunlight with a man. I had been divorced for exactly one year (separated for six months before that), and this was the first person I met who I thought I could have feelings for. We lived on different ends of the country, and we were discussing whether or not to have a long-distance relationship. He said, "Don't you want someone to come home to every night?"

If I had answered, my answer would have been *No*. But how was I to say that? How was I to tell this man, who I was hoping to be involved with, that I didn't want someone to come home to every night? That I only wanted someone to occasionally come home to? That I wanted to hear this man's voice on the phone, but not in my home? That I mostly wanted to have someone to think about? That I only wanted to see him every month or two? That I wanted to spend *some* nights with him wrapped around me, but, on most nights, I wanted to sleep alone? That sleeping alone had brought me the first peace I'd felt in a long time, and I was not ready to let that peace go? How was I to tell him that my son complicates things? That I am not looking for a father for my son?

That I am not looking for a man to step into that role until we are all ready? That maybe I will never be ready?

Maybe I could have told him about my ex-husband, about how he moved so quickly, about how I lived in a tiny apartment, and he would leave things behind as though it was *his* apartment too, and soon, I gave him a chair to leave those things on, then a drawer, and then, he was just there. And once he was there, I no longer was. I fit myself into the space my ex left for me, but it wasn't enough. Maybe I could have told this man that, for *most of my life*, I felt as though I had been fitting myself into the shape of other people.

I didn't tell this man any of that, though—not on that day, at least. A year later, we had the same discussion. This time I was honest. I told him that a long-distance relationship felt safe to me. I told him of how I had collapsed into my ex. I had only recently found myself again, and I didn't want to be lost anymore. I started to cry, and this man said, "Oh, Kelly," and drew my head to his chest, held my hair tenderly. This was the first time I let him see me cry in that way, and I think he thought I was crying over him, but my tears were not for him. My tears were for the version of myself that had been lost, for the version of myself he would never know.

I was quiet later that night, and he asked me, "Kelly, are you sad?"

"No," I said. "I'm annoyed with you." I was annoyed that he was not willing to try and meet me halfway, to have a relationship despite my limitations.

He was silent, then, not angry, but he hadn't expected that answer. Neither of us had expected that answer. Maybe the answer came because I had broken my pattern of helplessness. The discussion itself had been a rupture of my usual patterns.

One thing I have learned about patterns is that I can only change my own.

Years ago, I went to a writer's conference in Los Angeles. The sunshine was so golden, and the people so friendly. I was happier than I had been in a long time.

I ran into a poetry professor from Boise State (where I met my ex-husband while he was in his MFA). She said, "We're going to need a nonfiction person at Boise State, but you probably don't want to come back to Boise." I thought of that because, *of course, I want to go back to Boise*. I want to be closer to my family, to my friends, and I want to be back in the West. I would love to be in Boise, but how could I return to the place of my ex-husband's MFA? How could I do that?

She then told me a story of how two of my ex's friends had found out about my memoir. They were first shocked that my contract was with a Big Five publisher, then wondered what my ex must think. I realized I cannot go back to a community where the default reaction is not how happy they are for me. Instead, the default reaction is *to think about my abuser's feelings*.

The truth, I think, is that those men didn't know how to break their patterns of thinking about a perpetrator's consequences rather than the victim's because those men can't help but identify more with perpetrators.

I'll never forget how one of my ex's friends, a somewhat prominent writer in Boise, said to me, *I shared your essay and helped you,* as though I needed his help, as though I didn't earn the success that had come to me, as though that was the kind of help that I wanted from him when the only kind of help I wanted from the men in my abuser's life was for them to cut off contact with him. That rarely happened.

I'll never forget how another one of my ex's friends in Boise asked me to try to figure out *my triggers*, as though the abuse had been my fault, as though I had done something wrong.

I'll never forget how, the first summer my ex and I were apart, he flew with Reed to Boise. The day before they arrived, I drove the streets of Boise. I drove by the homes we had lived in. I sobbed in the car. Later that night, in the hotel, I called my ex. He answered. I told him I missed him; I didn't want him back, but I missed him.

He said, "I know. I miss you too." We were quiet for a long time. We still loved each other. Then, he said, "I'm going to go now."

"I know," I said. We never talked like that again.

The next day I picked up Reed at the airport. We went swimming by ourselves in a huge hotel pool. It was cold, and I was so lonely.

That writer—the one who *shared my essay and helped me*—along with the woman who questioned *my triggers*—threw a party for my ex, so while I was grieving alone in a hotel with the child I was mostly raising on my own, my ex was having a party thrown for him. I'd had to change my entire life in order to survive, but my abuser was able to continue living his life as before.

✲ ✲ ✲

The next day of the conference in LA, I was invited to a VIP party with important writing industry people. I am shy and do not like to do things alone, particularly things where everyone seems very good-looking, educated, and *New York*. In the past, I would have avoided the gathering altogether, or tried to pretend like I was having a good time, then left early. But I tried something different. I broke my pattern. I simply said, "I would love to come, but I am really shy." The publisher who invited me understood and took me under her wing. She introduced me to people, made me feel comfortable, and I had a genuinely great time.

I had already made plans for that night with a friend who I met while living in Boise (but who now lives in LA), so I took that friend with me to the party. This friend is also experiencing a lot of success, and her agent was there. Her agent asked how we had become friends, and my friend said, "Well, we met in Boise. Kelly was married to her abusive ex, and we weren't really friends at that time, but then, her ex-husband's friend raped me, and we bonded over having survived those dudes." We both laughed. Maybe only other abuse survivors can understand the humor in that, but there is something liberating in being able to laugh at exactly *how fucked-up that kind of connection is*.

Then, as my friend and I drank expensive Los Angeles drinks for free while talking to New York publishers and agents, we discussed how neither my abuser, nor her rapist, would ever have the experience we were having because they were not only abusers but untalented. There we were, my friend and I—two survivors and feminists—and, in that moment, our lives were so good, while both of our abusers continued to be hateful, violent men. We cheered to being free of them.

I don't know her patterns, but so many of mine have been broken. We have both worked so hard for autonomy—as artists and as women. Neither of us is living in the shape of anyone else.

Most of my life at that time didn't look like a VIP party in Los Angeles. Most of it looked like this—I was in a Western Sizzling parking lot in West Virginia. The sky gray, chemical factories sizzling by the side of the highway, and I had picked up Reed, who spent the weekend with his father. Reed sat in the backseat and told me how his uncle had yelled at his cousin. Reed sometimes has a hard time opening up to me, but this time, he couldn't stop talking. His uncle was yelling so loudly that Reed was scared. Reed wanted to end the argument, so he stood with his hand over the light switch. He wondered if he should turn off the lights. He told me of how his hand shook over that light switch.

He said, "Mom, I was shivering." I know that *shiver*. It comes from the inside. It comes from the bones. It comes from the little boy who hid in his bed while the dogs climbed in beside him and his father beat his mother in the next room over. It comes from *that little boy who will always be a part of Reed,* who will always be the source of that shiver.

Reed said his uncle finally noticed him and said, "Reed, maybe you should go into the other room," so Reed did.

I wanted to scream at his uncle the words that I will never be able to scream at him, which are "Don't you see how traumatized my little boy has been? How can you scare him like that?"

Then, Reed said, "I mean, I know [my uncle] is just preparing [my cousin] to be an adult."

I pulled over at that, and Reed and I went into a diner. I bought him a cheeseburger. I told him that children do not need that kind of *preparation*. I told him I left his father for exactly that reason. I told him that anger and violence is not okay, and that I left Reed's father so he wouldn't grow up with that. I told him about a time when I was still married, when Reed's cousin was in trouble for something that seemed like normal toddler behavior to me. I told him how Reed's uncle had us all go and play in the backyard, but he left the cousin, who was only four at that time, crying on the couch for an entire hour. I told Reed how I pretended like I had to go to the bathroom, but went in and sat with my nephew. I hugged him and told him what a good boy he was and how much I loved him. He quieted then, and I held him for a long time.

I don't know if I should have told Reed this story, but I did. I said, "The best thing you can do for your cousin is to continue to be a good friend to him."

Reed said, "Can I tell [my cousin] that story about you sneaking in to hug him?"

I said, "Oh, honey. He's probably forgotten, and I think it might just hurt him more to be reminded of it."

Reed said, "I just thought he might like to know he was loved. I don't think he thinks anyone loves him."

My heart broke because I no longer get to love my former nephew. I no longer get to advocate for him in the small ways I could before. Reed was quiet for a while, then said, "At least [my cousin] will know not to treat his own kids that way because his dad was like that, right?"

I was honest that sometimes people learn how to behave from their parents and treat their children the same way they were treated, but we all have the ability to break those patterns. Reed looked at me and said, "I'm glad you're the one raising me. When I have kids, I'm going to treat them the way that you treat me. I'm going to be patient and love them."

I can't save my former nephew. I can't save my ex's childhood self. I can't save my own childhood self. I don't even know if I can save my own child, but I have to try. Reed will break the patterns his father and I have given him.

I saw that man from the deck again. I wasn't strong enough to break the pattern entirely, and the following summer, when we were in the same place, I let him embrace me. That was the last time though. I'd like to say I was stronger than that, and I would break an unhealthy pattern the moment I identified it, but I didn't always. Sometimes patterns are broken in an instant, and sometimes, they're broken in bits and pieces over time. If we're lucky though, our lives will be long enough for us to make the changes we need to make.

A friend once said to me, "Kelly, life is short, but life is *long* too," and she was right. When I was being abused, I was convinced my life would be short. Maybe I even *wanted* my life to be short, but it kept getting longer, and the longer it got, the more I found myself breaking my self-destructive patterns. This has been such a gift, and what a gift it is to know that my son will have even more time than me. The potential is limitless.

The Answer Is in the Wound

A good friend was recently in a relationship with someone she recognized as abusive. He hadn't yet been abusive to her, but she saw his temperament in the way he treated his ex-wife. He was also dismissive of my friend's work, her creativity, and her talent. Most abuse doesn't start out as recognizable abuse. Instead, it starts out as little things that make their partners feel small:

You could be pretty if you tried. Your writing is so popular, but mine is literary. That's great that you were nominated for that award, but you probably won't get it; it usually goes to someone more prestigious. I'm not as physically attracted to you as I have been to other women, but I love the way you communicate.

That man taught my friend to feel small, so I wrote to her, "You are so beautiful, inside and out. You deserve someone who can mirror that back to you." I meant it.

She wrote back, "I reached out to you because you're the strongest person I know." She thought I had good boundaries with my lovers, that I no longer accepted mistreatment.

Maybe it was my public persona that led her to believe this, but I replied, "I am not strong," then heard my own words come back to me: *You are so beautiful, inside and out. You deserve someone who can mirror that back to you.*

Eight years ago, I fell in love with a man who didn't love me back. I loved him for two years, but I told myself I didn't, that I was in control. I believed he taught me how to *not* fall in love. I thought that, because he didn't destroy me, I must not have loved him. At the time, love that didn't destroy wasn't real to me. In time, I came to realize I had loved him, that though he wasn't in love with me, he was kind to me, and he respected me. He taught me what it feels like to be with someone stable and consistent. He didn't destroy me. He nourished me, and though I felt heartbreak when we parted, I left him more whole and more loving. Love didn't have to destroy me to be real.

The day before I was scheduled to defend my dissertation, I was diagnosed with the Type A flu that had turned into pneumonia. There was no way to reschedule my defense and graduate on time, so the next morning, I woke up, put on a nice top and cardigan—added a little lipstick for emphasis—and defended my dissertation via Skype from my upstairs office. I passed.

Dr. Sundberg.

I went downstairs, called my parents to celebrate, then went back to bed. I felt my fever rise as I slept. That night, the fever crested and waned. At its peak, it was 103.7 degrees. I thought, *If I die here tonight, my son will find me in the morning.* I thought, *I cannot die here tonight.* I didn't die that night, but I also didn't wake up the same.

* * *

Things were hard when I left my ex-husband, but once I realized I was moving on, that I was really doing it, my life became imbued with a sense of purpose, a sense of hope. There was always the potential of what was to come, and what was to come looked so very bright. First, I got into a PhD program. Then I started publishing essays and receiving awards. Then I got an agent. Then I got a book deal. Then we sold the translation rights. And so on, and so on.

And somehow, in the midst of all of that work, my personal life trudged along with me. I dated some. I had sex with older people. I had sex with younger people. I dated very casually. I tried to date more seriously and failed. Others congratulated me on my vulnerability. *Look at you,* they said. *You have been through so much, but you are still putting yourself out there.* I believed them. I believed I had successfully moved on.

Still, when I awoke from that flu, my body had an agitation to it. My fever dreams had enough pitch and intensity to both scare and excite me. I saw things—not real things—but *things,* and I woke up from that flu feeling extremely sensitive. My premonitions from childhood had returned. My fear of ghosts, too. And my night terrors. What that fever unearthed for me was my trauma. I had not buried it deep enough.

I knew then that I was still wounded—not in my brain, but in my body. My brain could rationalize my trauma, could usually recognize when I was distorting or overreacting, but my body only knew how to feel from the inside. To this day, what lives inside of me is darker and more unsettling than anything coming from the outside, and I have not again allowed myself to feel such confidence as I did before I was sick.

Shortly after I had the flu, a friend gifted me a session with an intuitive who called herself an emotional alchemist. She said to me, "Your heart is golden. It is so big and wonderful, but because of that, you feel things on a large scale, too. We need to give you some tools for protection."

I repeated to myself, "My heart is golden." I believed it.

Still, later, she brought up shame, and I sobbed. I said that my abusive marriage had brought out the worst in me, that I had accessed my own cruelty in the process of trying to protect myself, that I worried I was a bad person. She told me to look in the mirror—to really look at myself—and to say, "Thank you. I'm sorry. I love you. Forgive me."

Around that time, I wrote in my journal, "The truth is that, when I end up in a committed relationship, that person is going to have to be pretty special. They will need to be kind, funny, stable, and emotionally intuitive. And I can't imagine myself with someone who doesn't have their own kind of damage. I can only imagine myself with someone whose sore spots don't rub against mine because only a damaged person can understand the beauty in a certain kind of darkness."

I met R three months later.

An Akashic Records reader told me that my spirit chose my burdens in this lifetime in order to grow, but I don't want to believe that. It feels like a self-betrayal, as though I'm victim blaming myself. There were lessons to be learned through my experience, but I don't think I needed to learn them through violence. She also told me that there is something in me that brings up other people's trauma for them, that they see something in me they recognize, which forces them to confront their own wounds. This, I do believe. I have become accustomed to mirroring the pain of others back to them. This is not the kind of mirror I want to be; I want to be a mirror to their beauty. Maybe this is the lesson my spirit has chosen to learn in this lifetime.

When I was a girl, my friends and I played Bloody Mary in the darkened bathroom of the ranch house where I grew up. We spun each other around and shouted, "Bloody Mary! Bloody Mary! Bloody Mary!" When we opened our eyes, we only ever saw our own reflections. Somehow that was even more frightening.

Today is the day after Christmas. The day after my forty-sixth birthday. The day after the anniversary of the first time my then husband beat me. Christmas has historically caused me so much pain. This year, Christmas came and went without incident. My son was with his father's family, and my sweetie, R, made breakfast for me. He gave me the exact presents I wanted. We had great sex in the afternoon. Then he made me dinner, we watched a movie, and we went to bed. There was no fighting, which felt like a quiet miracle. Maybe the part of me that always wants to fuck something up has actually calmed down?

I don't know. All I know is that, when R looks at me, I see so much of my own goodness reflected back at me. No one has ever made me feel like this before, and though it saddens me to have had to wait for it for so long, I'm grateful for this gift: this mirror.

After that first time my husband beat me, I looked in the mirror for a long time. There was no outward evidence of what had happened. He was careful to only hit me where it wouldn't be visible. My face was red and swollen, but not from bruising. It was swollen from tears. As I stared at my reflection, I could have sworn someone else was looking back at me, and maybe she was.

R wasn't always a good boyfriend. He did a lot of things wrong. He'd never been in a serious relationship before, and he didn't think he was capable of it. For that reason, he didn't try very hard. The very least a person can do in a relationship is try.

Still, I could see the capacity in him to be a good partner to me, and I was mostly a good partner to him. I was loyal and supportive and showed up for him when he needed it. He said I was his mirror, showing him both where he was failing and where he was capable. He found it uncomfortable. If we're willing to grow, it's not so scary to see the bad stuff mirrored back to us, but he wasn't willing to grow at that time.

Eventually I fatigued of mirroring his failures to him, and I said, *No more*. I'd like to say that was when he changed, but he didn't. He broke up with me instead. A few months later, he wrote to me in a letter, "You helped me grow." Very little has made me angrier than reading that letter.

I ripped it up and texted him, "I was not put on this planet to help you grow."

* * *

I once had an acquaintance on social media who was going through a depressive episode and would post selfies of her crying. The pictures were grotesque, her face contorted in pain. It was uncomfortable to witness her suffering from the comfort of my living room. There was a part of me that didn't understand why she was doing it. Still, another part of me knew she just wanted to be seen.

There is a difference between being a witness to something and *witnessing* something. To *witness* is to see, to believe, and to accept without judgment. In my years of speaking out about domestic violence, I have had the opportunity to witness countless people. This is not a burden but a gift. Maybe this is the lesson my spirit has chosen to learn in this lifetime.

I'm trying to write a hopeful essay, and I *am* hopeful. Yet, I'm sitting here crying. There can be just as much grief and fear in hope as there is in the absence of it.

After tearing up his letter, I didn't speak to R for months, but he eventually asked if he could come by, and I relented. I had missed him. We had a beautiful day together, and at the end of it, I said, "We don't need to know exactly where things are going as long as we can grow together. Do you want to grow together?"

He did, and we've been growing together for a long while now. A year and a half ago, he moved in, and with my son, we're growing as a family. A *family* is something I didn't think I'd ever have again.

The truth is that I wasn't always a good partner to R either. I was a traumatized partner. I was distrustful, impatient, mean even. I'd lose my temper for no reason, then expect him to hold me while I wept in shame.

When Gabby Petito, the young woman who was murdered by her boyfriend in Wyoming, was still only *missing*, I made the mistake of reading the comments on an article at the *Washington Post*. Like all survivors, I already knew she was dead. Because the Utah police had erroneously identified her as the assailant, commenters kept calling her the abusive one. They were almost gleeful. *See, women can be abusive too! See? See? See?*

Triggers rarely happen when you're anticipating them. They sneak up unexpectedly like that flu had. And so, looking back at the afternoon when I read the comments about Gabby Petito, I can identify that there was a tension in my body and a panic in my heart. I was remembering when people had called *me* the abuser. Remembering when the police officer asked my abuser, "Did she hit you? Because we can arrest her, too." Remembering being turned so upside down emotionally that I, too, wondered if I was the abusive one. Remembering my own father telling me he didn't know what to believe.

I was remembering all of those things, but I wasn't remembering them in my brain. I was remembering them in my body, and the memories made me feel as though I was going to explode. The anger and anguish and sadness had to go somewhere. I should have gone for a walk. Journaled. Called a friend. I should have done one of the many healthy things that a trauma survivor should do in an instance like that, but that's not what I did. What I did was call R at work and yell at him that he wasn't a good partner to me, that his not being a good partner to me made me feel unsafe, and that I deserved to feel safe with the person I loved.

In the moment, I believed all of those things, and he was confused but patient. He couldn't tell me what I needed to hear because he didn't know what I needed to hear. Even I didn't know what I needed to hear. I hung up on him and wailed into the silence of my living room. I knew almost immediately that I was unequivocally wrong. I texted him that we could talk that evening when he was finished with work, and when we talked, I was contrite. I explained to him that I had been triggered. I was convinced he would end the relationship. It was the first instance in which my trauma had put a very serious wedge between us, but he forgave me.

The thing about R is that he's not the most emotionally intuitive, but he pays attention and he learns. I'm nearly positive that he has a list of my triggers somewhere: "Kelly gets triggered by the national news. Kelly gets triggered by victim blaming." Months later, during the Amber Heard and Johnny Depp trial, he trod lightly around me, but I, too, had learned, and I went into the news about that trial with my mental armor in place. Like I said, the thing about triggers is they rarely happen when you're anticipating them.

My psychic therapist once told me, "The answer is always in the wound. You have to look inside of it to find what you need." So, I did. I have looked inside of this wound in every which way possible. What I have discovered is the beauty in the darkness. It is a gift to know how dark the world can be and still be able to thrive in it. I spent my life fearing the darkness, but the darkness has made me who I am.

Early in my relationship with R, we had traveled to my home state together and stayed at a fancy hotel. We put on the white hotel robes and took a picture of ourselves in the mirror—sunburned and happy and in love. Even in that moment—the real one—not the picture or the memory of the moment—I saw us as a snapshot, a facsimile, a reflection. *Reflections aren't real*, I told myself. *This isn't real.* I thought suffering was the only thing that was real, that joy was an illusion.

From the moment I met R, I have been waiting for the relationship's end. Anticipating it. Predicting it. Trying to make it happen even. I know he has done the same because he and I share some of the same issues, even if the reasons for those issues are different.

Still, as terrified as I am, I'm also hopeful. I always thought I'd be worthy of love when I stopped being fucked-up. I spent years trying to make myself perfect—physically, intellectually, and emotionally—and that was one of the grandest failures of my lifetime. And yet this person, this *also-flawed* person, loves me exactly as I am. R has taught me that I can be messy and still be lovable.

* * *

My friend ended the relationship with the abusive man. She didn't end it immediately, but she did eventually. It can be so hard to do what we know is right when what we know is right goes against what we desire, but she did it.

She is one of the strongest people I know.

I think of looking in the mirror and saying to myself, "Thank you. I'm sorry. I love you. Forgive me." I wanted to believe it, but I didn't. I wish I was a person who had learned to love myself before finding love with someone else, but I don't know that I'll ever know how to love myself, and the only thing I can do is forgive myself for that.

Still, if I can be myself and still be loved, then what kind of freedom is contained within that? If R and I are not wasting our time trying to be other people, then how far can we grow together? Maybe into entire other lifetimes. Maybe into infinity. Maybe this is the lesson my spirit has chosen to learn in this lifetime. Maybe the lesson is the mirror itself.

Victim Impact Statement

When my ex-husband threw the bowl that broke my foot and ended my marriage, the judge dismissed his domestic battery charges with one caveat: He had to write a letter of apology to me. The letter arrived via certified mail. It was a master class in the passive voice.

I'm sorry for the bowl that broke your foot. I'm sorry for the hurt that it caused you.

I called my friend. "As a writer," I said, "you'd think that he could have written something better."

"Kelly," my friend said, "I think this might have been the best writing of his life."

When I threw the bowl that broke the window of the bedroom I shared with R, the impact made the glass crack, splinter, then spread. Jewelry fell out of the bowl in a tumble onto the carpet. I stared at the glass; the jewelry scattered in heaps. It sparkled; this mess that I had made.

Beyond the glass of the window, the Ohio sun was setting. Red, yellow, and pink streaked across the sky in splashes. It was both beautiful and angry, and at the sight, I fell onto the bed and keened a low, hard cry.

* * *

After the window broke.

No wait, let me rephrase that because I will not be using the passive voice here. After *I* broke the window. After *I* broke the window. After *I* broke the window. After *I* broke the window. After *I* broke the window. After *I* broke the window. After *I* broke the window.

After I broke the window, I remembered that I will only ever be an *after*.

I threw the bowl because my ex-husband had lied so many times, but R lied only once, and yet, the pain felt exactly the same.

When my ex-husband was prosecuted, I was never asked to write a victim impact statement. I wasn't even told when the hearing would be—West Virginia is famously lax on domestic abusers. There is a part of me that wonders, if I'd been given the chance to tell him how much he'd hurt me in front of a jury of his peers, could I have walked out of that courtroom healed? There is another part that knows I didn't yet understand what the full impact even was because I still thought healing was a possibility.

After I broke the window, I was wild. Feral. Crying. I ripped at my shirt. R started to cry too and hugged me. "No, baby," he said. "Don't cry. I'm not worth this."

Even in that moment of possession—because that's how it felt—as though I was possessed by a demon—my rational brain was able to say, *He isn't worth this. No one is.*

It wasn't about him though. It was about me and how I was trapped in a timeline that another man had made for me. Suspended in a state where the past was present, the future was past, and all that mattered was what had happened in that moment before I threw the bowl—when I realized that R had lied. All that mattered was that it felt just like so many moments that had come before it, even though it wasn't one of those moments at all.

There is no greater vulnerability than losing complete control in front of another person. I try so hard not to lose control, but in intimate relationships, it's impossible. This impossibility makes me desperate to be loved for exactly who I am. Bowl thrower and all.

My son went through a period where he would come home from preschool and say, "Tomorrow is today."

I would say, "No, tomorrow is tomorrow, but today is today."

He would shake his head and say, "No, tomorrow is today." He would say it so decisively that, after a while, I quit arguing with him about it. Now, I wonder if he was onto something.

If I could have written a victim impact statement on the day I threw the bowl, it would have read something like this:

> *Time moves on for my ex-husband, and yet, I am trapped in this timeline where every day, my mind reenacts the horrors that he inflicted onto me. This timeline is extremely hostile to everything that represents progress: finding love again, trusting someone, marriage. I am in love*

with a man who is kind and gentle and patient, and yet, I pick fights with him, assume the worst of him, project my ex's failures onto him, and I am terrified that I will lose him because of this. Abuse is always about control, and my abuser got it. It has been ten years, and he still has control over me.

For years, I had nightmares that I was drowning. Dreams of being trapped in cold water. I could see my loved ones reaching for me, but they couldn't save me. All they could do was watch me die.

When my son was little, he told me he only died in his dreams when he was being a hero and dying to save someone else. It was just the two of us by then, and there were times when I thought I was like the hero in his dreams. My nightmares mostly stopped after I left his father. I'd already drowned in the immensity of what happened during my marriage. So many loved ones watched, but the girl who had married that man, who allowed him to hurt her again and again? That girl was swept away in the current. She died so I could live.

R has only known me in the *after*. The woman I am now is stronger, more confident, and more accomplished than the girl I was. I have spent a decade trying to integrate pieces of her into this new existence, so when he saw me on that bed in a heap, he was hurt and afraid, and dare I say, surprised? I could see it all over his face. It is a testament to how well I have masked my trauma that he was surprised, but it is also so exhausting to wear a mask. Sometimes even I forget that it's a mask.

When I felt the familiar wildness enter my body, all I could think was *I've done it again*, but even in my moment of wildness, I knew my response was not proportionate. In this timeline, I have difficulty discerning the difference between a lie and a fist. The content of his lie doesn't really matter. What matters is that R didn't cheat, didn't abuse me. What matters is that my abuser taught me that lies are dangerous. What matters is that I am unable to distinguish between a lie that's dangerous and a lie that's forgivable. What matters is that I did forgive R, but not before he got a glimpse of that drowning girl who resurfaced.

What matters is that, in that moment, he saw me for exactly who I was.

After throwing the bowl, I left the apartment, and when I returned, R had swept up the mess. With the exception of a thin crack on the inside windowpane, the room looked as though nothing had happened. Later, he joked, "Even when you're angry, you still throw like a girl." I laughed, and it felt wrong to laugh, but still, the laughter was a relief—like taking a deep breath after being suffocated. I knew then that he still loved me, bowl throwing and all.

Before R, I didn't know how to love someone. Loving someone meant letting them see me, all of me. Letting someone see me meant I had to tell them what I'd suffered, and then the telling became its own kind of reliving. Even now, there are moments when I think it would be easier to be alone, so I would never again have to explain to someone why I am the way I am, but if I want to be happy, I have to be willing to be seen, even in my worst moments.

R replaced the window. He never called me "crazy" or treated me like I was. He was gentle with me, tender even. He had seen my very darkest self in my very darkest timeline, and though he might have been scared, he didn't run. That he stayed meant something. Maybe everything.

He has his own darkness, of course. We all do. Still, his darkness is nothing like the darkness of my abuser, and there is a part of me that wonders if it is R's own darkness that makes him approach mine with such generosity.

In the darkest timeline—the reenactment timeline—I am so hurt that I hurt everyone around me, but in this timeline, R shows me that his love is expansive enough to hold space for my hurt. For my shock and rage. For my bad bowl-throwing skills. For the drowning girl who cannot be saved. He can love her, not because of who she is, but because she is a part of who I am.

When I'm in this timeline—the present timeline—I can see things for how they really are. I can revise my victim impact statement.

He couldn't steal my life from me because I never belonged to him. Every time that I fought back, I fought for my own survival. Guess what? Here I am.

After I threw the bowl, I had another drowning dream. I was swept into a dark ocean, and when I surfaced, I couldn't see the shore so didn't know which way to swim. I felt a moment of panic, but even in my sleep state, something told me to relax and let the water take me where it wanted. It took me to the shore. I surfaced and stood on the beach watching the waves roiling, but the ground beneath my feet was solid. Then I woke up, and I turned and pressed my body to R's back. I wrapped my arm around him, and felt his heart beating like a drum underneath my palm. The rhythm was solid, steady, and stable. It lulled me back into a dreamless sleep where there was no pain, no shame, no regret. Nothing but our bodies resting quietly next to each other in the darkness.

The Blue of Melancholy

I was walking my dog at night, and the stars twinkled in a November sky that was cold, deep, and blue from moonlight. I've only ever seen stars like that in Columbus, Ohio, in the fall. In the summer, a haze obscures them, and in the winter, the clouds are oppressive and dreary. When I returned to my apartment, I could see my writing desk illuminated through the open blinds in the window. The contrast of the golden light in my office and the dark, frigid air outside brought me a sense of peace, and belonging, and also, a kind of sadness.

When I was a teenager in Idaho, I used to walk alone in the darkness almost every night. I lived in the kind of town where a girl could walk alone. The stars hung above me in a bright veil because the skies of the American West are so very clear. When I was under those big skies, my heart could crack open, and I could feel everything I had to repress at home and in school, where I couldn't be myself. I have never felt *less* alone than being alone under those big skies; it was a solace the landscape provided me, and I thought I would never leave.

I've lived in Montana, Oregon, West Virginia, and Ohio since then, and no matter where I am, fall makes me melancholy.

An English professor once described melancholy as "a sadness that we enjoy," and maybe this is why I love the color blue so much. The blue of night is a sadness that I hold dear.

When I was on the academic job market, I interviewed with a school in Utah. One of the interviewers said, "How would you support our students who want to publish with New York publishers?" I said, "I would tell them that it's not impossible, that I grew up just like your students, and no one ever told me that I could *be whatever I wanted to be*. That kind of mythology was reserved for other kids—kids who didn't grow up rural and poor."

As someone who grew up in the American West, I think of it as a place known for its inescapable beauty and loneliness. Also, ruggedness, lawlessness, individualism, an abundance of natural resources, and the exploitation of those natural resources and the people who exist within them. I also think of all of the ways in which I never quite fit there, though I longed to belong in the place that will, to this day, always be home to me.

A friend recently asked me if I knew a woman from my hometown who left and went on to become a successful writer, I told my friend I'd never heard of the woman, but it became clear from my Google searches the woman was part of a prominent ranching family in my community. I was surprised I had never heard of her. I told my friend, "Smart women from that area get punished when they leave." Maybe this is why I've felt lonely my entire life.

In her essay "The Blue of Distance," Rebecca Solnit writes about the blue sky on the horizon near the Great Salt Lake as the blue of desire. She says,

We treat desire as a problem to be solved, address what desire is for and focus on that something and how to acquire it rather than on the nature and the sensation of desire, though often it is the distance between us and the object of desire that fills the space in between with the blue of longing.

I remember reading that phrase—the blue of longing—and knowing precisely what the blue of longing is, though it would still be difficult for me to describe. Maybe it's that, once we have the object of our desire, it's so often no longer the thing we desire. Maybe it's that dreams are always at their brightest when they seem both possible and impossible at the same time.

In the years before my marriage, I found myself paralyzed by anxiety and perfectionism. I dropped out of college, then started classes again, then the cycle repeated. For someone who had always been told how smart I was, it was humiliating. I'd like to say I learned my lesson, but there were many other failures; there will be many more.

When I was in the ninth grade, I was one of only two girls who was cut from the high school volleyball team. That was one of my earliest humiliations. Still, the next day, I let a friend talk me into joining the cross-country team. I mostly did this because, on the cross-country team, I'd get to ride the bus with boys—my priorities were clearly those of a fourteen-year-old girl. I didn't get a boyfriend, and I was terrible at cross-country, but it ended up being some of the most fun I've had in my life. My mom would bring this up for years after as an example of my resilience. I would fail in some way, and she would say, "You're going to be okay. You're my daughter who, when you got cut from the volleyball team, joined the cross-country team."

Years later, after I had left my abusive marriage, I was crying on the phone to my mom. I didn't know what I was going to do—didn't know how I was going to support my child, how I was even going to make it from day to day. My mom said to me, "You're going to be okay. You're my daughter who, when you got cut from the volleyball team, joined the cross-country team."

I paused for a long while then said, "Mom, getting cut from the volleyball team was humiliating."

She didn't know how to respond, so she didn't, and she stopped bringing up that story, but as happens with stories like this, when she stopped bringing it up, I missed it. The tale had been a reminder of my failure, but it was also a reminder of my mother's faith in me. What I grew to learn in the years following was that I *was* resilient. That I *was* my mother's daughter who got cut from the volleyball team, then joined the cross-country team, and there was no shame in that. When my son was born, I became serious about my schooling and finished college, then I decided to get an MFA in creative writing, and shortly after that conversation with my mom, I divorced my husband and left our home in West Virginia to raise my child alone and start my PhD.

It was during my PhD when I finally began to write my own story, and though raising a child alone while getting a PhD was painful and difficult, it was the first time in my life where I was doing exactly what I wanted to be doing. I discovered that, when I listen to my heart rather than the voices of those around me, I'm not so lonely, even when I'm alone.

During my first two years of the PhD program, I drove all the way to Idaho and worked for the US Forest Service in the wilderness while my son spent weeks at his dad's and with my parents. The third summer, I still went home to Idaho, but I had been accepted to a writer's residency in Belgium. I had sold my book to a Big Five publisher on a proposal and received an advance to support me while I wrote it. It was a dream I had never been told was possible. Like I said, no one had ever told me I could be *whatever I wanted to be.*

I took a Greyhound bus from my hometown to Salt Lake City to catch my flight to Amsterdam, and I read Maggie Nelson's *Bluets* on the bus. Outside the windows of the bus, the Rocky Mountains and cerulean-blue skies flew by, and as we drove by the Great Salt Lake, I thought of Solnit's blue of longing. So much like melancholy.

I read from *Bluets,* "I have spent a lot of time staring at this core in my own 'dark chamber,' and I can testify that it provides an excellent example of how blue gives way to darkness—and then how, without warning, the darkness grows up into a cone of light." In that moment, I was living in my own cone of light. For the first time, I was safe, and doing what I loved.

I will never be grateful for my abusive marriage, but my life, as it is now, wouldn't exist without that marriage, and this life is a good one. My marriage was miserable, but the conditions of it—moving to West Virginia, deciding to get an MFA while my then husband worked, having my beautiful son—opened doors I never imagined opening for me.

After I left my marriage, a poet, who had been married for many years, told me that she had been married once before. She said, when that marriage ended, she felt like her entire life ended with it. Still, in time, she began to think of that marriage only as her "first, short marriage." I didn't believe that would ever happen for me, but now, I have been divorced for longer than I was married, have found someone new, have built a career, and have raised my son into an adult. As much as the darkness was a home during my marriage, I know now it was always going to explode into a cone of light because the darkness was only my *first, short marriage*, and I am the light.

While I was at the writer's residency in Belgium, I walked on a path every night. The blue of the sky was so different from the blue skies I had grown up with—softer, dimmer—as though it was "light seen through a veil" (as Henry Thoreau would have called it). One night, I looked at some thick cumulus clouds, and a line from an Amy Lowell poem flashed into my head: "Over the street the white clouds meet and sheer away without touching." I had failed so many times in my life, but all of those failures had brought me to this place. I went back to my room and wrote at my little desk that overlooked a field full of ponies while the sun dipped behind the horizon, and the blue faded to black.

In the final chapter of my memoir, there is a moment where I'm feeling happy while hanging out with a friend after a long period of grief. In that moment, both as it happened, and as I wrote it, I tried to memorize the outline of my happiness so I'd have it to return to when I felt sad. Mostly, I tried to memorize the outline of those blue, western skies. And it worked. Though I don't live in the West anymore, I'll always have those skies in my heart, but I also have so much more than blue in my heart now.

You Are the Star

Maggie says to me, "I want a relationship that brings me more joy, more peace, and more stability. Is that too much to ask?" I think of that word "more." The implication being that her life is already joyful, peaceful, and stable, and her life is because Maggie is, as the psychic therapist calls her, a "grown-up." The psychic therapist means spiritually, of course, and she has never said the same to me because I am not a grown-up. How can I be so broken and be a spiritual grown-up? The broken little girl I was is still living there inside of me. Still, I am, at the least, grown-up enough now to tend to her. I call back to her through the years, and I tell her that she is lovable, good, and worthy of care. I feel her call back to me. She thanks me, and I thank her too. I thank her for surviving so that I could be here, in this moment, where I am in love and getting remarried, and this love feels nothing like the loves of my past. It is a love with more joy, more peace, and more stability.

I am not religious, but in the past year, I have felt this blessing. It has been difficult for me to finish this book because I no longer feel so raw, spiritually hungry, and desperate, and for so many years, it has been that spiritual hunger that has fueled my creativity. I am now tasked to find a new kind of hunger—one that doesn't eat me alive but nourishes me instead.

This is not about my being saved by "love" or the "love of a good man." My mother says to me, "Kelly, R is a real prize," and she says it with a long look afterward. I interpret that look to mean "Don't fuck it up," and it annoys me because *I* am the prize. I was not saved by his love. I saved myself, and by saving myself, I became a prize. When you're a prize, good people are going to love you. This is what I have learned.

It is March, and we are getting married in July. I can't know what will happen on that day, but let me tell you what it looks like in my imagination: I will make a ton of food, a Mediterranean spread because that is R's favorite, and we will push our kitchen table to one wall to make more space for mingling. Julie, who is a pastry chef, is going to make a lemon basil cake for us. We will drape a flower garland over the French doors that lead from our living room to our den, and underneath that garland, in our modest little townhouse, we will get married. Megan will officiate, and my son, Reed, and Keema will give toasts. Kat will read a poem. Reed's girlfriend and best friend will be there too because they are also our beloveds. This living room wedding will be small out of necessity, but our chosen family will be there. R bought a disco ball just for this occasion, and the disco lights and flowers will be our only decorations.

* * *

In *Waking the Tiger*, Peter Levine says that traumatic transformation enables us to "become more in tune with the passionate and ecstatic dimensions of life." Ecstasy is best expressed through dance, and though dancing is not a part of the plan for this wedding, as sometimes happens, we might end the evening that way. Either way, we will be in this home that we have made. It is a home full of joy and peace and stability, and while R and I commit to continue to grow together (because that is the only kind of commitment that I am willing to make now), we will be surrounded by the people we love the most. The lights from the disco ball will swirl around us, will form constellations on the walls, and those lights, the constellations, and all of the stars around us will be little beams of magic that whisper to me and everyone else, *You did this. You saved yourself. You are the star.*

How to Not Be Heartbroken

A friend asked a question today about how to *not* be heartbroken all of the time. When I thought of her question, I realized I had no answer because I *am* heartbroken all of the time. I am in love with someone who loves me well, and I have everything that I have ever wanted. Still, I move through the world as a heartbroken person. I feel the grief of the loves I've lost before, and I anticipate the grief of the loves I will lose someday. I carry this grief with me everywhere. It colors the way I see the world. It shapes the way I interact with others. It makes me who I am, for better or for worse. When a heart has been broken too much, it can never heal back together in just the right way. There will always be fault lines, waiting for seismic activity.

I am forty-six, and in the past six months, I had a hysterectomy, I resigned from my tenure-track job, my son graduated high school, I got married, and my son went to college. I think this could be called a midlife crisis, and it occurs to me that a midlife crisis is a privilege because, when I was merely trying to survive, there would have been no room in my life to make such life-changing decisions.

I let my body betray me for years before deciding to excise the source of my misery (my uterus) because I didn't have good health insurance, nor did I have the time to be away from work for a prolonged period. I let my job betray me for years before deciding to excise *that* source of my misery because I needed the money to support my son, and I couldn't move him across the country when he was so happy in his high school. And though I've wanted to get married for a while, I was afraid to marry and have my new husband's income affect my son's financial aid prospects.

But then things hit a catalyst. My job became oppressive enough to be abusive, and Rich said, "Quit your job, and I will support you while you figure things out." My son, who had worked so hard at his magnet high school, received a full-tuition scholarship to an excellent school, so Rich and I could get married (and I could be added to his health insurance), and then, my parents helped me pay for my hysterectomy. The changes were so hard, but all of it was so very necessary.

The week before my son left for college, I dropped him off, so that he could spend a couple of days with his father. He was taking all of his LEGOs to his father's house for his siblings. His father and I usually avoid making eye contact, but because he had to get out of the car to help carry the boxes, he looked at me and waved. It was fine. We are civil now. Almost friendly sometimes, but still, I felt something when we made eye contact. Repelled. This was the man who battered me. It is so hard for me now to see what I ever saw in him. Tangled within that repulsion was a kind of deep sadness that I couldn't understand and still cannot articulate.

I said goodbye to my son, told him I loved him, then drove away, and the grief overwhelmed me. My son will never be my baby again. He is a man, and while I love the man he has become, I grieve the child who will always be lost to me now. Parenting is a journey of loss. The child who is with me today will be gone tomorrow, and then every day is a continuation of that pattern. But then, there are the gifts—the new selves to be formed—the new versions of that child who I have yet to greet.

As I drove home, I felt grief, but I also felt overwhelmed by gratitude. There were things I loved about my son's father. I loved his humor, his intelligence, his insight, and his ability to make people feel seen. My son has all of those qualities. The things that I loved the most about my son's father are in my son, and my son would not be who he is if he did not have the exact father that he has. For that reason, I feel grateful for having met my son's father, even though he hurt me more than anyone should hurt another person.

I drove home to Rich—my husband who I would have never met if my divorce hadn't taken me to that little town in Ohio—and I tried to tell him how I felt—that I felt so sad, but also grateful. I teared up and said, "Reed wouldn't be who he is, and I wouldn't have you if I hadn't met my ex-husband." I said, "He hurt me so much, but I'm also grateful for this place that I've landed, and I wouldn't have landed here without him. It's confusing."

Rich said, "But you would have landed somewhere else."

He didn't understand. I don't want to have landed somewhere else. *I like where I am.* He teared up then too and said, "I wish you hadn't had to go through so much to get here." And ay, there's the rub, isn't it?

A couple of nights later, we had dinner with another couple, and the woman told me that she, too, had been in an abusive relationship. She said that she's so grateful for her husband now, but he can't understand what it's like to feel that kind of gratitude because he's never known what it's like to feel such despair. She'd put her finger on what had confused me so much.

Grief has a razor's edge to it, and on one side is heartbreak, but on the other is gratitude. I would never say that everyone finds gratitude on the other side of heartbreak. I can't say that. In general, I have no real interest in making lemons into lemonade. Still, sometimes, the world makes the lemonade for me, and I only know how to appreciate the sweetness when things have been sour for so long. I couldn't have the gratitude that I have now if I hadn't experienced so much heartbreak.

At the end of my last marriage, I was still so in love with my then husband, but I knew that what we had wasn't working. I remember saying that to him, and he knew it was true. He said quietly, "You'll find someone else."

"I'll never find someone else," I said. "But I think I'd rather be alone than be with you."

And I was alone—for a long time—for years, in fact. When I met Rich, in the year after I finished my PhD, I didn't think that I would ever fall in love with him. He was goofy, nerdy, and young, and I thought that we'd just hook up for a while before I moved to the next city. But then, years passed, and we loved each other, then we lived together, and now, we're married. Sometimes I wonder if I'm living in an alternate reality where this is *not real*. That's how *not real* it feels. I am not sure how Rich and I made it this far when both of us were so avoidant that it took us four and a half years to even move in together. We're both Capricorns, I guess, so we're loyal, and we don't give up easily.

There is a lot of anti-marriage sentiment in feminism these days, and I get it. Statistically, marriage benefits men more than women; there just isn't a way around that. A week or so before my wedding, I had drinks with some friends. We talked a bit about my wedding, and one of my friends said (not unkindly), "I can't believe that you're getting married again." I knew what she meant. She wasn't questioning my relationship. She was questioning the entire premise of marriage, and those kinds of questions are very valid. Why would someone who suffered as much as I did within the patriarchal institution of marriage want to do it again?

The answer is simple: I just still have hope.

I still have hope that it can be different this time. I still have hope that Rich and I can be equals. I still have hope that my son can have a father figure in his life who isn't critical and mercurial. I still have hope that I can be myself within the context of a lifelong partnership. I still have hope that a partnership like this can last for a lifetime. I just still have a whole lot of hope.

The night before my first wedding, I cried in my parents' kitchen, and my mother hugged me and said, "You don't need to do this." But I did need to do it. Something in me—a soul contract maybe—needed to do it, needed to enter into that partnership with a man who would hurt me, needed to co-parent a child with him, needed to exit that partnership in the most painful way possible, and then, needed to learn how to love and trust again.

It is so hard to love and trust when someone has been through what I've been through, but here I am, and to be completely honest, I can't say that my trust is at 100 percent. I'm still working on that part. But my hope is at 100 percent.

This time, the night before my second wedding, there were no tears. No nerves. I slept soundly because, even if this marriage doesn't last—and I know that I'm not supposed to say that, but when you've been through what I've been through, it's hard not to think of it—I'll be okay. I'll be okay because Rich would never hurt me like my ex hurt me. I'll be okay because I've been through the worst, and I survived. I'll be okay because my son is becoming his own person, and I can see in him that *he'll be okay*.

In the first year that I lived in this apartment—the apartment where we had our little living room wedding a couple of months ago—I talked to Chrissy, a psychic. I was scared for my future—starting a new job, moving my child again, and trying to figure out how I would survive. Chrissy was alarmingly accurate. She told me that I would be too progressive for the conservative Christian institution I was teaching at, but that the sweetness of my students would be a gift (and oh how true this was!). She told me that Reed "is kind of accidentally popular wherever he goes, and he'll be okay" (and oh how true this was!). She even told me that Reed might end up in online school, which I thought would never happen (but oh how true this was!). She told me that my ex-husband would divorce again (oh how true this was!). She told me that I "couldn't disappoint Bob" (my cat), and a few years later, after he'd died unexpectedly from mouth cancer, I found the notes from that session in a journal, read those words, and cried because I'd needed to hear them. She also told me (about Rich), "Not being abusive is not enough," and that I didn't need to be so scared to introduce him to Reed—that I was waiting more for myself than for Reed.

I remember later telling Rich that "not being abusive is not enough" when I realized that I wasn't getting enough from him. I might have even admitted that I'd stolen the line from a psychic, but either way, he listened. He started to give me more, and eventually, it was everything (even more than) I needed. I also remember telling myself that Reed would be okay if he met the man in my life, and then being so thrilled when they turned out to genuinely like each other.

Reed gave the sweetest toast at our wedding (in his socks because it was that kind of wedding), and I was so touched and overwhelmed that I can't remember all of it, but he did such a wonderful job. He was confident, and funny, and articulate. He mostly talked about Rich—about how he first felt like Rich was a part of our family when he made banana bread French toast for Reed and his friend—about how Rich's sense of humor is really dumb, and how I act like I don't like it (but I secretly love it)—about how Rich and I are very different from each other, but it works because we complement each other.

Toward the end, he said that he realized he'd talked more about Rich than me, but that it's harder to talk about me. He said, "My mom and I have been through a lot," and though he is a very stoic person, for a moment, I thought his eyes misted over. He said we'd had so many changes in his lifetime, but he thought moving to Columbus was the best thing that had ever happened to us, and he joked, "I mean, let's be honest, you guys getting married is probably the smallest change in our lives right now!" This is true. Then he looked at me and thanked me for waiting so long to bring someone into his life. He thanked me for always putting him first. I bawled through the entire thing.

I'm glad that I waited for so long too. I might have been waiting more for myself than I was for Reed, but it was for the best. I wouldn't trade those years that Reed and I had alone for anything. They were some of the best years of my life, and the relationship that we have now is so much stronger because of it. When I told Reed that Rich and I were thinking of getting married, I asked if that was okay with him. "Why are you asking me?" he asked.

"If it's not," I said, "I won't marry him."

"Mom, it's okay with me. I think it's clear that Rich cares about you a lot," he said. "And it's clear that he cares about me too." That was all I needed to hear.

Months later, we had our little living room wedding. It was more of a party than a wedding, and that was my dream. A big, fun, comfortable celebration, surrounded by our beloveds. Rich and I have built something beautiful, and months later, after the wedding, the hope is still there.

I couldn't take Reed to college on move-in day because I had Covid. Reed's father offered to take him, but Reed said he'd rather have Rich take him. Rich is not a father to Reed, but he is a friend, and a friend was what Reed needed.

After they left, I let myself out of my room where I had been isolating, and I was feeling okay, so I started cleaning the apartment, and it was then that it hit me that my son was *gone*. I moved around the house in a frenzy, vacuuming, wiping down counters. I even cleaned the windows, and I bawled the entire time. Big sobs that came from my belly. I had thought that I was prepared for Reed to leave, and he went to a school that's only half an hour away, but there is really no way to prepare for the moment the love of your life moves out of your home. And he is. Reed is the love of my life.

It was an adjustment for Rich and me to have the house to ourselves. Rich, too, was surprised by how much he missed Reed, but we're managing. We don't hear from Reed all the time, but he quietly texts us his Wordle scores every day, so that I know he's alive. Because my job right now is primarily my writing, I'm home alone during the days, and at first, the silence and solitude felt oppressive, but after a while, it started to feel like such freedom. I have my health, I have my love, and my son is thriving at a wonderful college. I had to hustle for so many years, and I know I'll have to hustle again, but for now, I get to take a pause. I can catch my breath.

When I was cleaning on the day that Reed moved, I found a photo from his very first day of kindergarten. He was in the backyard of the house we'd shared with his dad, wearing a blue plaid shirt, Converse sneakers, and holding a Lightning McQueen lunchbox with the sweetest smile on his face. When I dropped him off at school that day, I saw him waiting in the line to get into the school, and he was so little and scared. I didn't want to let him go then either, but I had no choice, and it was fine. I remembered that day while looking at that photo, and all I could think was: *We went through so much, but we made it. We really made it.*

Acknowledgments

I am deeply indebted to the many journals where versions of these essays first appeared. "It Was Once like This Before" appeared in *The Collagist*. "Mornings, on the Ranch" appeared in *The Los Angeles Review*. "Mates" and "Spoons" appeared in *Gulf Coast*. "Poppies" and "What Sustains Me" appeared in *The Rumpus*. "The Sharp Point in the Middle" appeared in *PANK*. "Whirling Disease" appeared in *Denver Quarterly*. "When You Blame Amber Heard, You Blame Me Too" and a different version of "Still Screaming" appeared in *Guernica Magazine*. "The Witching Hour" appeared in *Alaska Quarterly Review*. "Every Line Is a Scream" and "Ritchie County Mall" appeared in *GayMag*. "Couplet" appeared in *The Journal*.

Thank you to Roxane Gay for seeing my vision for this book and making it happen. Roxane, you do so much good for the world—both literary and otherwise—and I am honored to be one of many recipients of your generosity.

To Joy Tutela—my agent, my mentor, and my friend. There is nothing I can say that could possibly convey how grateful

I am for these years of working with you, so all I can say is thank you.

Thank you to the Roxane Gay Books Fellows, Irena Huang and Clara Tamez, for your meticulous eyes and tireless work on behalf of Roxane Gay Books authors. Thanks, also, to Kelly Winton for the beautiful cover design, as well as Toni Burns Busot for a careful and thorough copyedit.

My writing community is large and wonderful, and this book has been a decade in the making, so I can't possibly thank everyone who has helped in some way with this book, but special thanks to Maggie Smith, Megan O' Laughlin, Kat Saunders, Rebecca Cuthbert, Heather Frese, Keema Waterfield, Sara Lucas, Melissa McCrae, and Mo Daviau.

Thank you to Patri Thompson for sending the best care packages when I needed them the most.

Thank you to Dinty W. Moore, Marisa Siegel, Megan Stielstra, and Ashley Ford for your support, mentorship, and encouragement.

Much gratitude to Melissa Ferrone, who collaborated with me on a previous version of the essay that became "Still Screaming."

Caroline Temple, you gave me the title to this book, and you helped to keep me sane. You change lives, and you changed mine. Thank you.

Thank you also to Chrissy Tolley for spiritual guidance over the years.

The Ohio Arts Council and the Greater Columbus Arts Council generously funded parts of this project, and for that, I am so grateful.

My parents, Eugene and Kathy, gave me the gift of using my voice, and there is no greater gift than that. Thank you, Mom and Dad. I love you.

To my brother, Glen, thank you for making me laugh and helping me to keep it real.

Rich, no one has ever supported me in achieving my dreams as much as you have. I am so grateful that I asked you what your sign was all of those years ago at The Union, and I'm even more grateful that you answered with Capricorn. I hope we keep growing together for the rest of our lives.

And finally, to Reed: The greatest honor of my life has been getting to be your mom. I couldn't be prouder of who you have become. Thank you for trusting me with my version of our story. I hope I've done it justice, and if you ever want to tell your version of our story, I hope I give you the same grace that you've extended to me. I love you forever.

Bibliography

Ahmed, Sara. "Hearing Complaint." Essay. In *Complaint!*, 1st ed., 1–2. Durham, NC: Duke University Press, 2021.

Boyer, Anne. "The Animal Model of Inescapable Shock." Poem. In *Garments Against Women* 67, 1st ed., 67:1–2. The New Series. Boise, ID: Ahsahta Press, 2015.

Dickinson, Emily. "One Need Not Be a Chamber to Be Haunted." In *Poems by Emily Dickinson: Three Series, Complete*, Edited by Todd, Mabel Loomis, and T.W. Higginson. Poem, 359. London, England: Read & Co., 2021.

Herman, Judith L. "Chapter One: The Rules of Tyranny." Chapter. In *Truth and Repair: How Trauma Survivors Envision Justice*, 1st ed., 36–37. New York: Basic Books, 2023.

Herman, Judith. "Disconnection." Chapter. In *Trauma and Recovery: The Aftermath of Violence—From Domestic Abuse to Political Terror*, 3rd ed., 52. New York: Basic Books, 1992.

Lady Bird. Film. Italia: Universal Pictures, 2018.

Levine, Peter A. "Chapter Five: Healing and Community." Chapter. In *Waking the Tiger: Healing Trauma*, 1st ed., 58. Berkeley, CA: North Atlantic Books, 1998.

Levine, Peter A. "Chapter Three: How Trauma Affects the Body." Chapter. In *Healing Trauma*, 35. Louisville, CO: Sounds True Adult, 2008.

Lowell, Amy. "Spring Day." Poetry Foundation. Accessed November 29, 2024. https://www.poetryfoundation.org/poems/53772/spring-day-56d233626c49b.

Nelson, Maggie. *Bluets*, 18, 56. Seattle, WA: Wave Books, 2009.

Olsen, Tillie. Essay. In *Silences*, 1st ed., 18. New York: Feminist Press, 2003.

Smith, Stevie. "Not Waving but Drowning." Poem. In *Best Poems of Stevie Smith*, 67. New York: New Directions, 2014.

Solnit, Rebecca. "The Blue of Distance." Essay. In *A Field Guide to Getting Lost*, 1st ed., 30. New York, New York: Penguin Books, 2005.

Thoreau, Henry David, and Damion Searls. *The Journals of Henry David Thoreau, 1837–1861*. New York, London: New York Review; Frances Lincoln distributor, 2009.

Vachss, Alice S. *Sex Crimes: Ten Years on the Front Lines Prosecuting Rapists and Confronting Their Collaborators*. New York: Henry Holt, 1994.